The face of Madeleine, painted on the wooden floor of a bar in Central City,
Colorado, as a tribute to d'Arcy's famous poem.
(Courtesy of the Central City Opera House Association.)

FAMOUS POEMS
FROM
BYGONE DAYS

EDITED AND
ANNOTATED BY

Martin Gardner

DOVER PUBLICATIONS, INC.
New York

Published in Canada by General Publishing Company, Ltd., 30 Lesmill Road, Don Mills, Toronto, Ontario.
Published in the United Kingdom by Constable and Company, Ltd., 3 The Lanchesters, 162–164 Fulham Palace Road, London W6 9ER.

Bibliographical Note

Famous Poems from Bygone Days is a new anthology, first published by Dover Publications, Inc., in 1995.

Library of Congress Cataloging-in-Publication Data

Famous poems from bygone days / edited and annotated by Martin Gardner.
 p. cm.
 ISBN 0-486-28623-1 (pbk.)
 1. English poetry. 2. American poetry. I. Gardner, Martin, 1914– .
PR1175.F225 1995
821'.008—dc20 94-48822
 CIP

Manufactured in the United States of America
Dover Publications, Inc., 31 East 2nd Street, Mineola, N.Y. 11501

A Verseman's Apology

Alas! I am only a rhymer,
I don't know the meaning of Art;
But I learned in my little school primer
To love Eugene Field and Bret Harte.
I hailed Hoosier Riley with pleasure,
To John Hay I took off my hat;
These fellows were right to my measure,
And I've never gone higher than that.

The Classics! Well, most of them bore me,
The Moderns I don't understand;
But I keep Burns, my kinsman, before me,
And Kipling, my friend, is at hand.
They taught me my trade as I know it,
Yet though at their feet I have sat,
For God-sake don't call me a poet,
For I've never been guilty of that.

A rhyme-rustler, rugged and shameless,
A Bab Balladeer on the loose;
Of saccharine sonnets I'm blameless,
My model has been—Mother Goose.
And I fancy my grave-digger griping
As he gives my last lodging a pat:
"That guy wrote McGrew;
'Twas the best he could do" . . .
So I'll go to my Maker with that.

—ROBERT SERVICE, from *Songs of a Sun-Lover*

CONTENTS

INTRODUCTION

THIS BOOK IS a companion to my *Best Remembered Poems,* published by Dover in 1992. In that collection I tried strenuously to select poems I thought were best known today among persons who find time to enjoy verse.

The poems here are different. They are poems that in the past were well known to American readers but that today are recalled, if at all, mainly by the elderly. For one reason or another most have fallen by the wayside. Like old popular verse still enjoyed, they are not to be confused with poems on the level of those by, say, Shakespeare, Milton or Keats. Yet they all have what so much of modern free verse lacks—that magic coincidence of easily comprehended significance with a pleasing sound structure.

Many of this book's poems are obviously close to what Robert Service, denigrating his own work, called "tootling, tin-whistle music." Even doggerel, however, can be relished, like the pleasure aroused by a well-drawn cartoon, or by jazz or by some country and gospel songs.

As in my previous anthology, selections are arranged alphabetically by author, with brief introductions to each. Don't be ashamed of being pleased or amused by these "humbler poets" whose sentimental songs, as Longfellow wrote in "The Day Is Done," gushed from their heart. Their lines are easy to memorize, and can be understood without revelations from erudite critics. Their rhythms may jingle and clank, but at least they have a melodic structure.

If you are as old as I am, many poems in this volume will awaken vague, half-forgotten memories. If you are young, you may find the poems as pleasantly surprising as hearing for the first time a catchy tune your great-grandparents warbled. The themes that dominate these poems of bygone days are: death (especially the deaths of infants and other loved ones), growing old, heaven, mother, father, grandparents, Jesus, church, preachers, recollections of childhood, the evils of drink, war and patriotism, farm life, tramps and vagabonds, ships and the sea, storms and railroads. Is it not curious that modern poets have little interest in cars and airplanes?

No stanzas in *Best Remembered Poems* are repeated here. Please do not write to ask why a certain gem has been omitted until you check

to see if it is in the earlier collection. Of course there are thousands of poems admired by our forefathers that are not in either anthology. All I can say is that I did my best to pick the few I believe were most admired.

In making selections I have relied heavily on my collection of pre-1900 "speakers" and huge anthologies that often have the word "gems" in their title. Particularly useful were the ten volumes of *The Speaker's Garland,* edited by Phineas Garrett, as well as collections of sentimental verse read on popular radio shows. I also made use of scrapbooks that I've picked up from time to time in antique malls. Is there any better proof of the nineteenth-century love of poetry than the practice of clipping and pasting down verse that appeared daily in almost every American newspaper? Alas, the snippers seldom recorded the date of a clipping or its source.

Not many people today, I suspect, are aware of how enormously admired poetry was in the days before motion pictures and television. It was read, savored, recited and memorized by persons on all levels of education and sophistication. England's great romantic poets were world famous and well paid. When Browning was the rage, his verse was studied in hundreds of Browning clubs in England and America. Professional reciters drew huge audiences all over the land. Hundreds of "speakers" were published, many illustrated with amusing photographs of men and women in elocutionary poses.

Before free verse took over, the love of poetry was also reflected in the high quality of song lyrics by George Gershwin, Cole Porter, Irving Berlin and many others, not to forget England's immortal Gilbert and Sullivan. Today's rock lyrics are so banal as to make "Ben Bolt" seem to have been penned by Shakespeare. Who can even understand the words of a rock song, often consisting of a single sentence shouted over and over while the singer gyrates and leaps about the stage to music that has little to offer except a few chords and an insistent beat?

The old love of poetry continued well into the early decades of this century, when Rudyard Kipling, Robert Service, Ella Wheeler Wilcox and Eddie Guest were widely read. When radio offered more than popular music and call-in talk shows, millions enjoyed such verse reciters as Tony Wons and Ted Malone.

Please do not imagine that I selected poems on the basis of vague impressions that they were once enormously admired. They are here as the result of considerable research into old anthologies and private scrapbooks to identify those poems that most often caught the fancy of anthologists and scrapbook keepers.

For help on several introductions I wish to thank William Harmon, professor of English at the University of North Carolina, Chapel Hill, and Russell T. Barnhart, New York City. It was Russell who located the obituaries of Edward Paramore, Jr. and Carlyle Fahlsworth Straub. I also acknowledge here my debt to Hayward Cirker, president of Dover Publications and an old friend, for proposing gems I otherwise would have overlooked, for valuable corrections and suggestions, and for encouraging me to assemble the two anthologies.

Three references deserve special mention: *Famous Single Poems,* by Burton Stevenson; *Victorian Parlour Poetry* (1992 Dover rpt. of *Parlour Poetry: A Casquet of Gems,* New York: The Viking Press, 1969) by Michael Turner; and *You Know These Lines!* by Merle De Voro Johnson. Johnson's book has a marvelous foreword by H. L. Mencken. The Baltimore sage allows that most of the old poems are "on all fours with cigarette pictures or college yells," but confesses that when he rereads them he begins "to wobble, for they take me back to happy days."

> Sound me the first line of any of them, and I'll rattle on to the last—lifted all the while as I have never been lifted by the metaphysical dithyrambs of T. S. Eliot. Is Eliot a better poet than Whittier or Holmes? I suppose he is. But let him prove it by wringing the human heart as they did. In particular, let him wring it so that it will stay wrung.

JOHN QUINCY ADAMS
(1767–1848)

BORN IN BRAINTREE (now Quincy), Massachusetts, the son of the second president of the United States, John Quincy Adams became the sixth president. As Secretary of State he was responsible for the Monroe Doctrine.

Not many know that Adams was a professor of rhetoric at Harvard, his alma mater, and that he was a writer of copious prose and verse. A portion of his diary was published in twelve volumes!

Only one poem, "The Wants of Man," became famous. It is said to have first been published in an Albany newspaper, though I do not know the details, and can be found in Adams's *Poems of Religion and Society* (1848). Its twenty-five stanzas are seldom given entire. The first two lines are quoted from Oliver Goldsmith's *The Hermit*, which appears in *The Vicar of Wakefield* (1766).

The Wants of Man

"Man wants but little here below,
　Nor wants that little long."
'Tis not with *me* exactly so;
　But 'tis so in my song.
My wants are many and, if told,
　Would muster many a score;
And were each wish a mint of gold,
　I still should long for more.

What first I want is daily bread—
　And canvas-backs—and wine—
And all the realms of nature spread
　Before me, when I dine.
Four courses scarcely can provide
　My appetite to quell;
With four choice cooks from France beside,
　To dress my dinner well.

What next I want, at princely cost,
　Is elegant attire:
Black sable furs for winter's frost,
　And silks for summer's fire,
And Cashmere shawls, and Brussels lace
　My bosom's front to deck,—
And diamond rings my hands to grace,
　And rubies for my neck.

1

And then I want a mansion fair,
 A dwelling-house, in style,
Four stories high, for wholesome air—
 A massive marble pile;
With halls for banquetings and balls,
 All furnish'd rich and fine;
With high-blood studs in fifty stalls,
 And cellars for my wine.

I want a garden and a park,
 My dwelling to surround—
A thousand acres, (bless the mark!)
 With walls encompassed round—
Where flocks may range and herds may low,
 And kids and lambkins play,
And flowers and fruits commingled grow,
 All Eden to display.

I want, when summer's foliage falls,
 And autumn strips the trees,
A house within the city's walls,
 For comfort and for ease;
But here, as space is somewhat scant,
 And acres somewhat rare,
My house in town I only want
 To occupy—a square.

I want a steward, butler, cooks;
 A coachman, footman, grooms;
A library of well-bound books,
 And picture-garnish'd rooms;
Corregio's *Magdalen* and *Night*,
 The *Matron of the Chair;*
Guido's fleet coursers in their flight,
 And Claudes, at least a pair.

I want a cabinet profuse
 Of medals, coins, and gems;
A printing-press for private use,
 Of fifty thousand ems;
And plants, and minerals, and shells;
 Worms, insects, fishes, birds;
And every beast on earth that dwells
 In solitude or herds.

Here it is:

OK final:

(apologies — producing clean version now)

I want a board of burnish'd plate,
 Of silver and of gold;
Tureens of twenty pounds in weight,
 And sculpture's richest mould;
Plateaus, with chandeliers and lamps,
 Plates, dishes—all the same;
And porcelain vases, with the stamps
 Of Sèvres and Angouleme.

And maples of fair glossy stain,
 Must form my chamber doors,
And carpets of the Wilton grain
 Must cover all my floors;
My walls with tapestry bedeck'd,
 Must never be outdone;
And damask curtains must protect
 Their colours from the sun.

And mirrors of the largest pane
 From Venice must be brought;
And sandal-wood and bamboo cane,
 For chairs and tables bought;
On all the mantel-pieces, clocks
 Of thrice-gilt bronze must stand,
And screens of ebony and box
 Invite the stranger's hand.

I want (who does not want?) a wife,—
 Affectionate and fair;
To solace all the woes of life,
 And all its joys to share.
Of temper sweet, of yielding will,
 Of firm, yet placid mind,—
With all my faults to love me still
 With sentiment refined.

And as Time's car incessant runs,
 And Fortune fills my store,
I want of daughters and of sons
 From eight to half a score.
I want (alas! can mortal dare
 Such bliss on earth to crave?)
That all the girls be chaste and fair,
 The boys all wise and brave.

And when my bosom's darling sings,
 With melody divine,
A pedal harp of many strings
 Must with her voice combine.
Piano, exquisitely wrought,
 Must open stand apart,
That all my daughters may be taught
 To win the stranger's heart.

My wife and daughters will desire
 Refreshment from perfumes,
Cosmetics for the skin require,
 And artificial blooms.
The civet fragrance shall dispense,
 And treasured sweets return;
Cologne revive the flagging sense,
 And smoking amber burn.

And when at night my weary head
 Begins to droop and doze,
A chamber south, to hold my bed,
 For nature's soft repose;
With blankets, counterpanes, and sheet,
 Mattress, and sack of down,
And comfortables for my feet,
 And pillows for my crown.

I want a warm and faithful friend,
 To cheer the adverse hour;
Who ne'er to flatter will descend,
 Nor bend the knee to power,—
A friend to chide me when I'm wrong,
 My inmost soul to see;
And that my friendship prove as strong
 For him as his for me.

I want a kind and tender heart,
 For others' wants to feel;
A soul secure from fortune's dart,
 And bosom arm'd with steel;
To bear divine chastisement's rod,
 And, mingling in my plan,
Submission to the will of God,
 With charity to man.

I want a keen observing eye,
 An ever-listening ear,
The truth through all disguise to spy,
 And wisdom's voice to hear:
A tongue, to speak at virtue's need,
 In heaven's sublimest strain;
And lips, the cause of man to plead,
 And never plead in vain.

I want uninterrupted health,
 Throughout my long career,
And streams of never-failing wealth,
 To scatter far and near—
The destitute to clothe and feed,
 Free bounty to bestow,
Supply the helpless orphan's need,
 And soothe the widow's woe.

I want the genius to conceive,
 The talents to unfold,
Designs, the vicious to retrieve,
 The virtuous to uphold;
Inventive power, combining skill,
 A persevering soul,
Of human hearts to mould the will,
 And reach from pole to pole.

I want the seals of power and place,
 The ensigns of command;
Charged by the People's unbought grace
 To rule my native land.
Nor crown nor scepter would I ask
 But from my country's will,
By day, by night, to ply the task
 Her cup of bliss to fill.

I want the voice of honest praise
 To follow me behind,
And to be thought in future days
 The friend of human kind,
That after ages, as they rise,
 Exulting may proclaim
In choral union to the skies
 Their blessings on my name.

These are the Wants of mortal Man,—
 I cannot want them long,
For life itself is but a span,
 And earthly bliss—a song.
My last great Want—absorbing all—
 Is, when beneath the sod,
And summoned to my final call,
 The *Mercy of my God.*

And oh! while circles in my veins
 Of life the purple stream,
And yet a fragment small remains
 Of nature's transient dream,
My soul, in humble hope unseared,
 Forget not thou to pray,
That this, THY WANT, may be prepared
 To meet the Judgment Day.

THOMAS BAILEY ALDRICH
(1836–1907)

BORN IN PORTSMOUTH, New Hampshire, Aldrich spent most of his life in New York City and Boston as a popular poet, novelist, essayist, playwright and author of short stories. He also edited several newspapers and magazines in the two cities, including the *Atlantic Monthly*, where he spent ten years as editor. His well-polished lyrics were collected in half a dozen volumes.

Aldrich intensely disliked the free verse of Walt Whitman, and Whitman had an equally low opinion of Aldrich's poems. "Yes, Tom," he once said, "I like your tinkles. I like them very well."

"Memory" was perhaps Aldrich's best known lyric. It was much admired by Whittier, who said it aroused "a pleasure that is very near pain in its intensity."

Memory

My mind lets go a thousand things,
Like dates of wars and deaths of kings,
And yet recalls the very hour—
'T was noon by yonder village tower,

And on the last blue noon in May
The wind came briskly up this way,
Crisping the brook beside the road;
Then, pausing here, set down its load
Of pine-scents, and shook listlessly
Two petals from that wild-rose tree.

ANONYMOUS

ANONYMOUS POEMS, as they traveled from one newspaper to another, underwent many changes. "The Hell-Bound Train" is no exception. I have taken a version that I found in an old scrapbook and combined it with the one in Hazel Felleman's *The Best Loved Poems of the American People* (1936). Felleman's version changes "Tom Gray" to "A Texas Cowboy," and includes three stanzas not contained in the scrapbook's clipping. Where lines differ, I have selected those that scan the best.

Granger's Index to Poetry says the poem has been attributed to J. W. Pruitte, but I have never seen it with this byline.

The Hell-Bound Train

Tom Gray lay on the bar room floor,
Having drunk so much he could drink no more.
So he fell asleep with a troubled brain,
And dreamed that he rode on a hell-bound train.

The engine with blood was red and damp,
And brilliantly lit with a brimstone lamp;
For fuel, an imp was shoveling bones,
While the furnace rang with a thousand groans.

The boiler was filled with lager beer,
And the devil himself was the engineer.
The passengers made such a motley crew—
Church members, Atheist, Gentile and Jew.

Rich men in broadcloth, beggars in rags;
Handsome young ladies and withered old hags;
Yellow and black men, red, brown and white—
All chained together! What a terrible sight.

While the train rushed on at an awful pace—
The sulphurous fumes scorched hands and face;
Wider and wider the country grew,
As faster and faster the engine flew.

Louder and louder the thunder crashed
And brighter and brighter the lightning flashed;
Hotter and hotter the air became
Till the clothes were burned from each quivering frame.

And out of the distance there arose a yell,
"Ha, ha," said the devil, "we're nearing hell!"
Then oh, how the passengers shrieked with pain
And begged the devil to stop the train.

But he capered about, and sang in his glee,
And laughed and joked at their agony.
"My faithful friends, you have done my work,
And the devil can never a pay-day shirk.

"You have bullied the weak, and robbed the poor,
And the starving brother turned from your door.
You have laid up gold where the canker rusts,
And given free vent to your fleshly lusts.

"You have justice scorned, and corruptions sown,
And trampled the law of nature down.
You have drank and rioted, murdered and lied,
And mocked at God in your hell-born pride.

"You have paid full fare, so I'll carry you through,
For it's only just you should get your due.
Why, the laborer always expects his hire,
So I'll land you safe in the lake of fire.

"Where your flesh shall roast in the flames that roar,
And my imps torment you forever more."
Then Tom awoke with an anguished cry,
Clothes soaked with sweat and his hair standing high.

And he prayed as never before that hour,
To be saved from drink and the devil's power,
And his vows and prayers were not in vain,
For he never more rode on a hell-bound train.

ANONYMOUS

I HAVE NO IDEA where this tender poem first appeared or who the author was. Burton Stevenson, in his monumental *Home Book of Verse* (1922), titles it "Forty Years Ago" and credits it to one Francis Huston, about whom he says he has no biographical information. Hazel Felleman, in *The Best Loved Poems of the American People* gives it the byline of Dill Armor Smith, whoever he is. *Granger's Index to Poetry* calls the author "unknown," and so does *The Fireside Book of Poetry* (1878), edited by Henry Coates, and *The Speaker's Garland*, 1, no. 3 (1872). Music for the poem, by William Willing, can be found in *Heart Songs* (1909).

I had a great-uncle who taught me the knife game mentioned in the fourth stanza. It is known as mumblety-peg or mumble-the-peg. A pocket knife is flipped off each finger, wrist, elbow, shoulder, chin and other parts of the body so that it falls and sticks in the ground. The loser is obliged to pull out with his teeth a peg that has been driven firmly into the dirt.

Twenty Years Ago

I've wander'd to the village, Tom, I've sat beneath the tree,
Upon the school-house play-ground, which shelter'd you and
 me;
But none were there to greet me, Tom, and few were left to
 know,
That play'd with us upon the grass some twenty years ago.

The grass is just as green, Tom—barefooted boys at play,
Were sporting just as we did then, with spirits just as gay;
But the "master" sleeps upon the hill, which, coated o'er with
 snow,
Afforded us a sliding-place, just twenty years ago.

The old school-house is alter'd some, the benches are re-
 placed
By new ones, very like the same our pen-knives had defaced;
But the same old bricks are in the wall, the bell swings to and
 fro,
Its music, just the same, dear Tom, 'twas twenty years ago.

The boys were playing some old game, beneath the same old
 tree—
I do forget the name just now; you've play'd the same with me

On that same spot; 'twas play'd with knives, by throwing so
 and so,
The loser had a task to do, there, just twenty years ago.

The river's running just as still, the willows on its side
Are larger than they were, Tom, the stream appears less wide;
But the grapevine swing is ruin'd now where once we play'd
 the beau,
And swung our sweethearts—"pretty girls"—just twenty years
 ago.

The spring that bubbled 'neath the hill, close by the spread-
 ing beech,
Is very low—'twas once so high that we could almost reach;
And kneeling down to get a drink, dear Tom, I even started
 so!
To see how much that I am changed since twenty years ago.

Near by the spring, upon an elm, you know I cut your name,
Your sweetheart's just beneath it, Tom, and you did mine the
 same—
Some heartless wretch had peel'd the bark, 'twas dying sure
 but slow,
Just as the one whose name was cut, died twenty years ago.

My lids have long been dry, Tom, but tears came in my eyes,
I thought of her I loved so well—those early broken ties—
I visited the old churchyard, and took some flowers to strew
Upon the graves of those we loved, some twenty years ago.

Some are in the churchyard laid, some sleep beneath the sea,
But few are left of our old class, excepting you and me,
And when our time is come, Tom, and we are call'd to go,
I hope they'll lay us where we play'd, just twenty years ago.

ANONYMOUS

SLASON THOMPSON, in his 1899 book *The Humbler Poets: A Collection of Newspaper and Periodical Verse 1870 to 1885*, includes this anonymous tearjerker. It would be interesting to know when and where it was first published. I have never seen it with a byline.

Guilty or Not Guilty

She stood at the bar of justice,
 A creature wan and wild,
In form too small for a woman,
 In features too old for a child;
For a look so worn and pathetic
 Was stamped on her pale young face,
It seemed long years of suffering
 Must have left that silent trace.

"Your name," said the judge, as he eyed her
 With a kindly look, yet keen;
"Is Mary McGuire, if you please, sir."
 "And your age?" "I'm turned fifteen."
"Well, Mary,"—and then from a paper
 He slowly and gravely read,
"You are charged here—I'm sorry to say it—
 With stealing three loaves of bread.

"You look not like an offender,
 And I hope that you can show
The charge to be false. Now, tell me
 Are you guilty of this, or no?"
A passionate burst of weeping
 Was at first her sole reply,
But she dried her eyes in a moment
 And looked in the judge's eye.

"I will tell you just how it was, sir;
 My father and mother are dead,
And my little brother and sisters
 Were hungry, and asked me for bread.
At first I earned it for them
 By working hard all day,
But somehow times were bad, sir,
 And the work all fell away.

"I could get no more employment;
 The weather was bitter cold;
The young ones cried and shivered—
 Little Johnny's but four years old;
So, what was I to do, sir?
 I am guilty, but do not condemn,

I took—oh, was it stealing?—
 The bread to give to them."

Every man in the court-room—
 Graybeard and thoughtless youth—
Knew, as he looked upon her,
 That the prisoner told the truth.
Out of their pockets brought 'kerchiefs,
 Out from their eyes sprung tears,
And out from old faded wallets
 Treasures hoarded for years.

The judge's face was a study,
 The strangest you ever saw,
As he cleared his throat and murmured
 Something about the law;
For one so learned in such matters,
 So wise in dealing with men,
He seemed on a simple question
 Sorely puzzled just then.

But no one blamed him, or wondered,
 When at last these words they heard:
"The sentence of this young prisoner
 Is, for the present, deferred."
And no one blamed him, or wondered
 When he went to her and smiled,
And tenderly led from the court-room
 Himself, the "guilty" child.

ANONYMOUS

THIS PLEASANT little lyric turns up in dozens of pre-1900 anthologies, never with a byline. Where the editors found it, who knows?

When Mamma Was a Little Girl

When mamma was a little girl
 (Or so they say to me)
She never used to romp and run,

Nor shout and scream with noisy fun,
 Nor climb an apple tree.
She always kept her hair in curl,—
When mamma was a little girl.

When mamma was a little girl
 (It seems to her, you see)
She never used to tumble down,
Nor break her doll, nor tear her gown,
 Nor drink her papa's tea.
She learned to knit, "plain," "seam," and "purl,"—
When mamma was a little girl.

But grandma says—it must be true—
 "How fast the seasons o'er us whirl!
Your mamma, dear, was just like you,
 When she was grandma's little girl."

MABEL DOW (NORTHAM) BRINE
(1816–1913)

I HAVE uncovered nothing about Mabel Brine beyond the fact that she was born in New York and the author of numerous books of short stories and verse, mostly for children. "Somebody's Mother," her one famous poem, first appeared in *Harper's Weekly* (March 2, 1878), and later in *Madge, the Violet Girl and Other Poems* (New York, 1881). An illustrated twelve-page edition of the poem, titled *Somebody's Mother,* was printed in Bavaria and distributed in America by Dutton in 1891.

I can't help recalling the joke about the boy scout who came home with a black eye. When his mother asked what happened, he said he had tried to help an old lady across the street, but she didn't want to go.

Somebody's Mother

The woman was old and ragged and gray
And bent with the chill of the Winter's day.

The street was wet with a recent snow
And the woman's feet were aged and slow.

She stood at the crossing and waited long,
Alone, uncared for, amid the throng

Of human beings who passed her by
Nor heeded the glance of her anxious eye.

Down the street, with laughter and shout,
Glad in the freedom of "school let out,"

Came the boys like a flock of sheep,
Hailing the snow piled white and deep.

Past the woman so old and gray
Hastened the children on their way.

Nor offered a helping hand to her—
So meek, so timid, afraid to stir

Lest the carriage wheels or the horses' feet
Should crowd her down in the slippery street.

At last came one of the merry troop,
The gayest laddie of all the group;

He paused beside her and whispered low,
"I'll help you cross, if you wish to go."

Her aged hand on his strong young arm
She placed, and so, without hurt or harm,

He guided the trembling feet along,
Proud that his own were firm and strong,

Then back again to his friends he went,
His young heart happy and well content.

"She's somebody's mother, boys, you know,
For all she's aged and poor and slow.

"And I hope some fellow will lend a hand
To help my mother, you understand,

"If ever she's poor and old and gray,
When her own dear boy is far away."

And "somebody's mother" bowed low her head
In her home that night, and the prayer she said

Was "God be kind to the noble boy,
Who is somebody's son, and pride and joy!"

THOMAS EDWARD BROWN
(1830–1897)

A PRIEST in the Church of England, Father Brown was born on the Isle of Man, and after studying at Oxford, taught at several boys' schools in England. He turned out at least five books of verse, and his *Collected Poems* was published posthumously in 1900. Much of his poetry was written in Manx dialect.

Only one lyric became famous, "My Garden." I can't resist following it with a parody by James Albert Lindon (1914–1979), my favorite British writer of comic verse. It appeared in *Yet More Curious & Comic Verse*, selected by J. M. Cohen (Penguin, 1959) and is included here with the author's permission.

My Garden

A garden is a lovesome thing, God wot!
 Rose plot,
 Fringed pool,
 Ferned grot—
 The veriest school
 Of peace; and yet the fool
Contends that God is not—
Not God! in gardens! when the eve is cool?
 Nay, but I have a sign:
 'Tis very sure God walks in mine.

My Garden (by J. A. Lindon)

A garden is a *lovesome* thing? What rot!
Weed plot,
Scum pool,
Old pot,
Snail-shiny stool
In pieces; yet the fool
Contends that snails are not—
Not snails! in gardens! when the eve is cool?
Nay, but I see their trails!
'Tis very sure *my* garden's full of snails!

ROBERT BROWNING
(1812–1889)

Best Remembered Poems included two Browning lyrics, "Meeting at Night" and "Pippa's Song." Perhaps even more admired and anthologized in the nineteenth century was "Prospice," a Latin word meaning "look forward." Written shortly after his wife's death, it is surely the greatest poem in English on how faith in immortality can combat a fear of dying. The poem was set to music by C. V. Stafford.

Prospice

Fear death?—to feel the fog in my throat,
 The mist in my face,
When the snows begin, and the blasts denote
 I am nearing the place,
The power of the night, the press of the storm,
 The post of the foe;
Where he stands, the Arch Fear in a visible form,
 Yet the strong man must go:
For the journey is done and the summit attained,
 And the barriers fall,
Tho' a battle 's to fight ere the guerdon be gained,
 The reward of it all.
I was ever a fighter, so—one fight more,
 The best and the last!
I would hate that death bandaged my eyes, and forbore,
 And bade me creep past.
No! let me taste the whole of it, fare like my peers
 The heroes of old,
Bear the brunt, in a minute pay glad life's arrears
 Of pain, darkness and cold.
For sudden the worst turns the best to the brave,
 The black minute 's at end,
And the elements' rage, the fiend-voices that rave,
 Shall dwindle, shall blend,
Shall change, shall become first a peace out of pain,
 Then a light, then thy breast,
O thou soul of my soul! I shall clasp thee again,
 And with God be the rest!

JOHN WILLIAM BURGON
(1813–1888)

MANY AUTHORS in this collection, and in my previous anthology, are remembered today, if at all, for just one single poem. Reverend Burgon is a "one-line poet." His fame rests solely on one line in his long and long-forgotten poem "Petra":

> A rose-red city half as old as Time.

Born in Smyrna, Turkey, Burgon grew up in England where he took holy orders at Worcester College, Oxford. For thirteen years he was vicar of St. Mary's, Oxford, and for twelve years until his death he was dean of Chichester. His numerous books include controversial Biblical studies, biographies and collections of sermons.

Petra was a mysterious ancient city in Jordan, near Mount Hor where Aaron died and was buried according to the biblical account in Numbers 20: 25–28. The ancient city of Petra is currently in the news because of recent archaeological digs. In 1990 a Byzantine church, rich in striking mosaics, was uncovered there, but the 2000-year-old city, of perhaps 30,000 inhabitants, remains buried under sand. (Steven Spielberg's *Indiana Jones and the Last Crusade* was filmed among the colorful ruins of Petra.)

Petra was the capital of the Nabatean pagan empire. The Nabatean kingdom, annexed by Rome in 106, was a flourishing trading center until it was reduced to rubble by violent earthquakes in 363 and 551. Muslims took it over in the seventh century.

Petra (Greek for "rock") is almost certainly the city called Selah in the Old Testament. The area is noted for its red sandstone mountains, its hundreds of sandstone caves and its stupendous tombs carved out of the rock. Their color gives the region the rosy hues noted in Burgon's famous line.

Lord Dunsany's short fantasy "The Expulsion" (in *The Fourth Book of Jorkens*) is about a nineteenth-century poets' club in London that expelled Burgon. The reason: a minor poet named Rogers (Samuel Rogers?) accused Burgon of stealing part of his line from a poem he (Rogers) had written: "By many a temple half as old as time." Burgon's ghost explains to Jorkens that he lifted the phrase without thinking: "Nobody steals jewelry out of a jeweler's shop," Burgon's shade says, just before fading away. "But if you see a fine brooch lying about on a grocer's counter among shavings of carrot and sticks of licorice, one is so surprised, that perhaps unconsciously—."

Burgon's poem won the Newdigate Prize at Oxford in 1845 and was published as a small book the following year. The final couplet of the excerpt given here was so widely quoted that many anonymous parodies circulated around England. James Sutherland, in his *Oxford Book of Literary Anecdotes* (1975), recalls a parody aimed at an aged Oxford don, The Reverend Thomas Short:

> Match me such marvel, save in college port,
> That rose-red liquor half as old as Short.

Petra (excerpt)

It seems no work of man's creative hand,
By labour wrought as wavering fancy plann'd,
But from the rock as if by magic grown,
Eternal, silent, beautiful, alone!
Not virgin-white like the old Doric shrine
Where erst Athena held her rites divine;
Not saintly-grey, like many a minster fane,
That crowns the hill, and consecrates the plain;
But rosy-red as if the blush of dawn
That first beheld them were not yet withdrawn;
The hues of youth upon a brow of woe,
Which man deemed old two thousand years ago.
Match me such marvel save in Eastern clime,
A rose-red city half as old as Time.

JOHN BURROUGHS
(1837–1921)

BURROUGHS' FAME RESTS, of course, on his many books of essays about nature. Born near Roxbury, New York, he had an early career as a school teacher, studied medicine for a while and worked as a bank examiner. His nature writing was done at his home on a fruit farm near Esopa, New York, in an isolated cabin he called Slabsides. A devoted friend of Walt Whitman, he wrote Whitman's first biography.

"Waiting" expresses Burroughs' secular pantheism. Like the great pantheist Spinoza, Burroughs believed that the future is predetermined—it has to be whatever it will be, so why not relax and stoically accept all that happens to you, both good and bad? He once said his poem was about Baptist predestination, "watered down or watered up."

Written when Burroughs was twenty-five, "Waiting" first appeared in the *Knickerbocker Magazine* (Vol. 61, 1863, page 201). He used it as a preface to his book *The Light of Day*, and later included it in his one book of verse, *Bird and Bough* (1906). Whittier, who knew the poem by heart, put it in his anthology *Songs of Three Centuries*.

Burton Stevenson, in *Famous Single Poems*, reveals that the original poem had an extra stanza between the fifth and last:

Yon floweret nodding in the wind
 Is ready plighted to the bee;
And, maiden, why that look unkind?
 For, lo! thy lover seeketh thee.

As Burroughs himself realized, dropping this stanza greatly improves the poem. Stevenson also discloses that later in life Burroughs added an equally mediocre stanza at the end of the poem. As far as I know, Stevenson was the first to publish it. I have never seen it elsewhere:

> The law of love threads every heart
> And knits it to its utmost kin,
> Nor can our lives flow long apart
> From souls our secret souls would win.

Waiting

Serene, I fold my hands and wait,
 Nor care for wind, nor tide, nor sea;
I rave no more 'gainst time or fate,
 For, lo! my own shall come to me.

I stay my haste, I make delays,
 For what avails this eager pace?
I stand amid the eternal ways,
 And what is mine shall know my face.

Asleep, awake, by night or day,
 The friends I seek are seeking me;
No wind can drive my bark astray,
 Nor change the tide of destiny.

What matter if I stand alone?
 I wait with joy the coming years;
My heart shall reap where it hath sown,
 And garner up its fruit of tears.

The waters know their own and draw
 The brook that springs in yonder height;
So flows the good with equal law
 Unto the soul of pure delight.

The stars come nightly to the sky;
 The tidal wave unto the sea;
Nor time, nor space, nor deep, nor high,
 Can keep my own away from me.

WILLIAM ALLEN BUTLER
(1825–1902)

ALTHOUGH WILLIAM BUTLER, an Albany-born New York City attorney and civic leader, wrote two novels, four biographies and scores of poems, he became a sterling example of the "one-poem poet"—a person remembered only for a single piece of doggerel.

"Nothing to Wear" appeared anonymously in *Harper's Weekly* (February 7, 1857). When the editor told Butler he needed twenty-four more lines to fill out the last page, Butler obligingly supplied them, though we don't know which lines they were. As usual with anonymous verse that makes an instant hit, several charlatans at once claimed to have written it, including a pesky teen-aged girl named Peck. Such claims faded after the poem appeared in Butler's book *Nothing to Wear: An Episode of City Life* (1857), with illustrations by Augustus Hoppin.

The poem was widely reprinted in America, England and France. It spawned endless imitations, parodies and book titles such as *Nothing to Do*, by Horatio Alger, and *Nothing to Say*, by Mortimer Thompson. No less a critic than William Dean Howells was so captivated by the poem that he praised it to the skies in an introduction to a collection of Butler's poetry. Howells called it a "new poem, flashing from a novel impulse . . . gay with lights and tints unknown before"—a ballad that "swept the country like a prairie fire." Septimus Winner set the poem to music, published in Philadelphia by Lee and Walker in 1857.

Flora MacFlimsey is mentioned in James Joyce's *Ulysses* on page 346 of the 1961 Vintage edition ("None of your spoilt beauties, Flora MacFlimsy sort, was Cissy Caffrey.").

Nothing to Wear
An Episode of City Life

Miss Flora McFlimsey, of Madison Square,
 Has made three separate journeys to Paris,
And her father assures me, each time she was there,
 That she and her friend Mrs. Harris,
(Not the lady whose name is so famous in history,[1]
But plain Mrs. H., without romance or mystery)
Spent six consecutive weeks without stopping,
In one continuous round of shopping;
Shopping alone, and shopping together,

[1] *Mrs. Harris . . . history*] Burton Stevenson, in a chapter on "Nothing to Wear" in *Famous Single Poems*, says that a Mrs. Harris lost her life in a tragic accident at Niagara Falls.

At all hours of the day, and in all sorts of weather;
For all manner of things that a woman can put
On the crown of her head or the sole of her foot,
Or wrap round her shoulders, or fit round her waist,
Or that can be sewed on, or pinned on, or laced,
Or tied on with a string, or stitched on with a bow,
In front or behind, above or below:
For bonnets, mantillas, capes, collars, and shawls;
Dresses for breakfasts, and dinners, and balls;
Dresses to sit in, and stand in, and walk in;
Dresses to dance in, and flirt in, and talk in;
Dresses in which to do nothing at all;
Dresses for winter, spring, summer, and fall;
All of them different in color and pattern,
Silk, muslin, and lace, crape, velvet, and satin,
Brocade, and broadcloth, and other material,
Quite as expensive and much more ethereal;
In short, for all things that could ever be thought of,
Or milliner, *modiste*, or tradesman be bought of,
From ten-thousand-francs robes to twenty-sous frills;
In all quarters of Paris, and to every store,
While McFlimsey in vain stormed, scolded, and swore,
They footed the streets, and he footed the bills.

The last trip, their goods shipped by the steamer *Arāgo*,
Formed, McFlimsey declares, the bulk of her cargo,
Not to mention a quantity kept from the rest,
Sufficient to fill the largest sized chest,
Which did not appear on the ship's manifest,
But for which the ladies themselves manifested
Such particular interest, that they invested
Their own proper persons in layers and rows
Of muslins, embroideries, worked under-clothes,
Gloves, handkerchiefs, scarfs, and such trifles as those;
Then, wrapped in great shawls, like Circassian beauties,
Gave *good-by* to the ship, and *go-by* to the duties.
Her relations at home all marveled no doubt,
Miss Flora had grown so enormously stout
For an actual belle and a possible bride;
But the miracle ceased when she turned inside out,
And the truth came to light, and the dry goods beside,
Which, in spite of Collector and Custom-house sentry,
Had entered the port without any entry.

And yet, though scarce three months have passed since the
 day
This merchandise went, on twelve carts, up Broadway,
This same Miss McFlimsey, of Madison Square,
The last time we met, was in utter despair,
Because she had nothing whatever to wear!

NOTHING TO WEAR! Now, as this is a true ditty,
 I do not assert—this, you know, is between us—
That she's in a state of absolute nudity,
 Like Powers' Greek Slave,[2] or the Medici Venus;
But I do mean to say, I have heard her declare,
 When, at the same moment, she had on a dress
 Which cost five hundred dollars, and not a cent less,
 And jewelry worth ten times more, I should guess,
That she had not a thing in the wide world to wear!

I should mention just here, that out of Miss Flora's
Two hundred and fifty or sixty adorers,
I had just been selected as he who should throw all
The rest in the shade, by the gracious bestowal
On myself, after twenty or thirty rejections,
Of those fossil remains which she called "her affections,"
And that rather decayed, but well-known work of art,
Which Miss Flora persisted in styling "her heart."
So we were engaged. Our troth had been plighted,
Not by moonbeam or starbeam, by fountain or grove,
But in a front parlor, most brilliantly lighted,
Beneath the gas-fixtures we whispered our love.
Without any romance, or raptures, or sighs,
Without any tears in Miss Flora's blue eyes,
Or blushes, or transports, or such silly actions,
It was one of the quietest business transactions,
With a very small sprinkling of sentiment, if any,
And a very large diamond imported by Tiffany.
On her virginal lips while I printed a kiss,
She exclaimed, as a sort of parenthesis,
And by way of putting me quite at my ease,
"You know, I'm to polka as much as I please,
And flirt when I like—now stop, don't you speak—

[2] *Powers' Greek Slave*] a famous statue by the then-popular American sculptor
Hiram Powers (1805–1873).

And you must not come here more than twice in the week,
Or talk to me either at party or ball,
But always be ready to come when I call;
So don't prose to me about duty and stuff,
If we don't break this off, there will be time enough
For that sort of thing; but the bargain must be
That, as long as I choose, I am perfectly free,
For this is a sort of engagement, you see,
Which is binding on you but not binding on me."

Well, having thus wooed Miss McFlimsey and gained her,
With the silks, crinolines, and hoops that contained her,
I had, as I thought, a contingent remainder
At least in the property, and the best right
To appear as its escort by day and by night;
And it being the week of the STUCKUPS' grand ball—
 Their cards had been out for a fortnight or so,
 And set all the Avenue on the tip-toe,—
I considered it only my duty to call,
 And see if Miss Flora intended to go.
I found her—as ladies are apt to be found,
When the time intervening between the first sound
Of the bell and the visitor's entry is shorter
Than usual—I found; I won't say—I caught her—
Intent on the pier-glass, undoubtedly meaning
To see if perhaps it didn't need cleaning.
She turned as I entered—"Why, Harry, you sinner,
I thought that you went to the Flashers' to dinner!"
"So I did," I replied, "but the dinner is swallowed,
 And digested, I trust, for 'tis now nine and more,
So being relieved from that duty, I followed
 Inclination, which led me, you see, to your door.
And now will your ladyship so condescend
As just to inform me if you intend
Your beauty, and graces, and presence to lend,
(All of which, when I own, I hope no one will borrow)
To the STUCKUPS', whose party, you know, is to-morrow?"

The fair Flora looked up with a pitiful air,
And answered quite promptly, "Why Harry, *mon cher,*
I should like above all things to go with you there;
But really and truly—I've nothing to wear."

"Nothing to wear! go just as you are;
Wear the dress you have on, and you'll be by far,

I engage, the most bright and particular star
 On the Stuckup horizon"—I stopped, for her eye,
Notwithstanding this delicate onset of flattery,
Opened on me at once a most terrible battery
 Of scorn and amazement. She made no reply,
But gave a slight turn to the end of her nose
 (That pure Grecian feature), as much as to say,
"How absurd that any sane man should suppose
That a lady would go to a ball in the clothes,
 No matter how fine, that she wears every day!"

So I ventured again—"Wear your crimson brocade,"
(Second turn up of nose)—"That's too dark by a shade."
"Your blue silk"—"That's too heavy;" "Your pink"—"That's
 too light."
"Wear tulle over satin"—"I can't endure white."
"Your rose-colored, then, the best of the batch"—
"I haven't a thread of point lace to match."
"Your brown *moire antique*"—"Yes, and look like a Quaker;"
"The pearl-colored"—"I would, but that plaguey dress-
 maker
Has had it a week"—"Then that exquisite lilac,
In which you would melt the heart of a Shylock."
(Here the nose took again the same elevation)—
"I wouldn't wear that for the whole of creation."
 "Why not? It's my fancy, there's nothing could strike it
As more *comme il faut*—" "Yes, but, dear me, that lean
 Sophronia Stuckup has got one just like it,
And I won't appear dressed like a chit of sixteen."
"Then that splendid purple, that sweet Mazarine;
That superb *point d'aiguille*, that imperial green,
That zephyr-like tarletan, that rich *grenadine*—"
"Not one of all which is fit to be seen,"
Said the lady, becoming excited and flushed.
"Then wear," I exclaimed, in a tone which quite crushed
 Opposition, "that gorgeous *toilette* which you sported
In Paris last spring, at the grand presentation,
When you quite turned the head of the head of the nation;
 And by all the grand court were so very much courted."
 The end of the nose was portentously tipped up,
And both the bright eyes shot forth indignation,
As she burst upon me with the fierce exclamation,
"I have worn it three times at the least calculation,
 And that and the most of my dresses are ripped up!"

Here *I ripped out* something, perhaps rather rash,
 Quite innocent, though; but, to use an expression
More striking than classic, it "settled my hash,"
 And proved very soon the last act of our session.
"Fiddlesticks, is it, Sir? I wonder the ceiling
Doesn't fall down and crush you—oh, you men have no
 feeling,
You selfish, unnatural, illiberal creatures,
Who set yourselves up as patterns and preachers.
Your silly pretense—why what a mere guess it is!
Pray, what do you know of a woman's necessities?
I have told you and shown you I've nothing to wear,
And it's perfectly plain you not only don't care,
But you do not believe me" (here the nose went still higher).
"I suppose if you dared you would call me a liar.
Our engagement is ended, Sir—yes, on the spot;
You're a brute, and a monster, and—I don't know what."
I mildly suggested the words—Hottentot,
Pickpocket, and cannibal, Tartar, and thief,
As gentle expletives which might give relief;
But this only proved as spark to the powder,
And the storm I had raised came faster and louder,
It blew and it rained, thundered, lightened, and hailed
Interjections, verbs, pronouns, till language quite failed
To express the abusive, and then its arrears
Were brought up all at once by a torrent of tears,
And my last faint, despairing attempt at an obs-
Ervation was lost in a tempest of sobs.

Well, I felt for the lady, and felt for my hat, too,
Improvised on the crown of the latter a tattoo,
In lieu of expressing the feelings which lay
Quite too deep for words, as Wordsworth would say;
Then, without going through the form of a bow,
Found myself in the entry—I hardly knew how—
On door-step and sidewalk, past lamp-post and square,
At home and up stairs, in my own easy chair;
 Poked my feet into slippers, my fire into blaze,
And said to myself, as I lit my cigar,
Supposing a man had the wealth of the Czar
 Of the Russias to boot, for the rest of his days,
On the whole, do you think he would have much to spare
If he married a woman with nothing to wear?

Since that night, taking pains that it should not be bruited
Abroad in society, I've instituted
A course of inquiry, extensive and thorough,
On this vital subject, and find, to my horror,
That the fair Flora's case is by no means surprising,
 But that there exists the greatest distress
In our female community, solely arising
 From this unsupplied destitution of dress,
Whose unfortunate victims are filling the air
With the pitiful wail of "Nothing to wear."
Researches in some of the "Upper Ten" districts
Reveal the most painful and startling statistics,
Of which let me mention only a few:
In one single house, on Fifth Avenue,
Three young ladies were found, all below twenty-two,
Who have been three whole weeks without any thing new
In the way of flounced silks, and thus left in the lurch
Are unable to go to ball, concert, or church.
In another large mansion near the same place
Was found a deplorable, heart-rending case
Of entire destitution of Brussels point lace.
In a neighboring block there was found, in three calls,
Total want, long continued, of camels'-hair shawls;
And a suffering family, whose case exhibits
The most pressing need of real ermine tippets;
One deserving young lady almost unable
To survive for the want of a new Russian sable;
Another confined to the house, when it's windier
Than usual, because her shawl isn't India.
Still another, whose tortures have been most terrific
Ever since the sad loss of the steamer *Pacific*,
In which were ingulfed, not friend or relation,
(For whose fate she perhaps might have found consolation,
Or borne it, at least, with serene resignation)
But the choicest assortment of French sleeves and collars
Ever sent out from Paris, worth thousands of dollars,
And all as to style most *recherché* and rare,
The want of which leaves her with nothing to wear,
And renders her life so drear and dyspeptic
That she's quite a recluse, and almost a skeptic,
For she touchingly says that this sort of grief
Can not find in Religion the slightest relief,
And Philosophy has not a maxim to spare
For the victims of such overwhelming despair.

But the saddest by far of all these sad features
Is the cruelty practised upon the poor creatures
By husbands and fathers, real Bluebeards and Timons,
Who resist the most touching appeals made for diamonds
By their wives and their daughters, and leave them for days
Unsupplied with new jewelry, fans, or bouquets,
Even laugh at their miseries whenever they have a chance,
And deride their demands as useless extravagance;
One case of a bride was brought to my view,
Too sad for belief, but, alas! 'twas too true,
Whose husband refused, as savage as Charon,
To permit her to take more than ten trunks to Sharon.
The consequence was, that when she got there,
At the end of three weeks she had nothing to wear,
And when she proposed to finish the season
At Newport, the monster refused out and out,
For his infamous conduct alleging no reason,
Except that the waters were good for his gout;
Such treatment as this was too shocking, of course,
And proceedings are now going on for divorce.

But why harrow the feelings by lifting the curtain
From these scenes of woe? Enough, it is certain,
Has here been disclosed to stir up the pity
Of every benevolent heart in the city,
And spur up Humanity into a canter
To rush and relieve these sad cases instanter.
Won't somebody, moved by this touching description,
Come forward to-morrow and head a subscription?
Won't some kind philanthropist, seeing that aid is
So needed at once by these indigent ladies,
Take charge of the matter? Or won't PETER COOPER[3]
The corner-stone lay of some splendid super-
Structure, like that which to-day links his name
In the Union unending of honor and fame;
And found a new charity just for the care
Of these unhappy women with nothing to wear,
Which, in view of the cash which would daily be claimed,
The *Laying-out* Hospital well might be named?

[3] *PETER COOPER*] American industrialist, inventor and philanthropist (1791–1883) who built Manhattan's Cooper Union to provide education for the city's working class.

Won't STEWART,[4] or some of our dry-goods importers,
Take a contract for clothing our wives and our daughters?
Or, to furnish the cash to supply these distresses,
And life's pathway strew with shawls, collars, and dresses,
Ere the want of them makes it much rougher and thornier,
Won't some one discover a new California?

Oh, ladies, dear ladies, the next sunny day
Please trundle your hoops just out of Broadway,
From its whirl and its bustle, its fashion and pride,
And the temples of Trade which tower on each side,
To the alleys and lanes, where Misfortune and Guilt
Their children have gathered, their city have built;
Where Hunger and Vice, like twin beasts of prey,
 Have hunted their victims to gloom and despair;
Raise the rich, dainty dress, and the fine broidered skirt,
Pick your delicate way through the dampness and dirt,
 Grope through the dark dens, climb the rickety stair
To the garret, where wretches, the young and the old,
Half-starved and half-naked, lie crouched from the cold.
See those skeleton limbs, those frost-bitten feet,
All bleeding and bruised by the stones of the street;
Hear the sharp cry of childhood, the deep groans that swell
 From the poor dying creature who writhes on the floor,
Hear the curses that sound like the echoes of Hell,
 As you sicken and shudder and fly from the door;
Then home to your wardrobes, and say, if you dare—
Spoiled children of Fashion—you've nothing to wear!

And oh, if perchance there should be a sphere,
Where all is made right which so puzzles us here,
Where the glare, and the glitter, and tinsel of Time
Fade and die in the light of that region sublime,
Where the soul, disenchanted of flesh and of sense,
Unscreened by its trappings, and shows, and pretense,

[4] *STEWART*] Alexander Turney Stewart (1803–1876), one of America's greatest retail merchants of the nineteenth century. A native of Ireland, he opened the nation's first department store in 1823 at 283 Broadway, in Manhattan. Its instant success led to larger and larger stores. His seven-story "marble palace" at Broadway and Chambers Street became the offices of the *New York Sun* from 1910 to 1950. Now in a state of decay, there are plans for restoring it as a city landmark. Garden City, Long Island, was developed by Stewart. At the time of his death, Stewart was building a charitable boarding facility for working women and girls.

Must be clothed for the life and the service above,
With purity, truth, faith, meekness, and love;
Oh, daughters of Earth! foolish virgins, beware!
Lest in that upper realm you have nothing to wear!

WILLIAM McKENDREE CARLETON
(1845–1912)

BORN ON A farm near Hudson, Michigan, Will Carleton's newspaper career began in nearby Hinsdale, Michigan, where he edited *The Standard,* a weekly paper, after graduating from Hinsdale College. Later he edited the Detroit *Weekly Tribune* before finally settling in Brooklyn as one of America's most admired writers of sentimental dialect verse.

Carleton's output was staggering. A trilogy of books containing farm poems (*Farm Ballads, Farm Legends* and *Farm Festivals*) was followed by a trilogy of books with poems about city life (*City Ballads, City Legends* and *City Festivals*). There were other verse collections and several unsuccessful plays.

"Over the Hill to the Poor-House," his most famous ballad, first ran in *Harper's Weekly* (June 17, 1871), and was included in *Farm Ballads* (1873). Readers were so distressed by it that Carleton cheered them up with a sequel, "Over the Hill from the Poor-House." Other happy endings were penned by other hands. (See, for example, May Mignonette's sequel in *Crown Jewels* [1887], edited by Henry Davenport Northrup [pages 48–49].) Carleton's second most admired ballad, "Betsey and I Are Out," told of a domestic spat. It, too, was followed with a happy ending, "Betsey and I Made Up."

Harper and Brothers published Carleton's poor-house poems in *Over the Hill to the Poor-House* (1904), a book illustrated with eight plates by W. E. Mears. In a preface to this edition Carleton wrote:

> Letters have often been written me by repentant sons and daughters, acknowledging their error of indifference to the parents who had reared and loved them, and stating that reparation had been made as far as possible. And it has not been seldom that poor-masters have reported a diminution in the number of their tenants, caused by the withdrawal of old people whose children were ashamed of their neglect.

Change "poor-house" to "nursing home" and the heart-rending sentiments of Carleton's famous poem are of course still with us.

In 1923 Michigan set aside October 21, the date of the poet's birth, as Will Carleton Day. "Over the hill" has become a common expression for a person who is past his or her prime. Whether it had its origin in Carleton's poem I don't know.

Over the Hill to the Poor-House

Over the hill to the poor-house I'm trudgin' my weary way—
I, a woman of seventy, and only a trifle gray—
I, who am smart an' chipper, for all the years I've told,
As many another woman that's only half as old.

Over the hill to the poor-house—I can't quite make it clear!
Over the hill to the poor-house—it seems so horrid queer!
Many a step I've taken a-toilin' to and fro,
But this is a sort of journey I never thought to go.

What is the use of heapin' on me a pauper's shame?
Am I lazy or crazy? am I blind or lame?
True, I am not so supple, nor yet so awful stout;
But charity ain't no favor, if one can live without.

I am willin' and anxious an' ready any day
To work for a decent livin', an' pay my honest way;
For I can earn my victuals, an' more too, I'll be bound,
If any body only is willin' to have me round.

Once I was young and handsome—I was, upon my soul—
Once my cheeks was roses, my eyes as black as coal;
And I can't remember, in them days, of hearin' people say,
For any kind of a reason, that I was in their way.

'Taint no use of boastin', or talkin' over free,
But many a house an' home was open then to me;
Many a han'some offer I had from likely men,
And nobody ever hinted that I was a burden then.

And when to John I was married, sure he was good and smart,
But he and all the neighbors would own I done my part;
For life was all before me, an' I was young an' strong,
And I worked the best that I could in tryin' to get along.

And so we worked together; and life was hard, but gay,
With now and then a baby for to cheer us on our way;
Till we had half a dozen, an' all growed clean an' neat,
An' went to school like others, an' had enough to eat.

So we worked for the child'rn, and raised 'em every one;
Worked for 'em summer and winter, just as we ought to 've
 done;
Only perhaps we humored 'em, which some good folks con-
 demn,
But every couple's child'rn's a heap the best to them.

Strange how much we think of our blessed little ones!—
I'd have died for my daughters, I'd have died for my sons;
And God he made that rule of love; but when we're old and
gray,
I've noticed it sometimes somehow fails to work the other way.

Strange, another thing: when our boys an' girls was grown,
And when, exceptin' Charley, they'd left us there alone;
When John he nearer an' nearer come, an' dearer seemed to
be,
The Lord of Hosts he come one day an' took him away from
me.

Still I was bound to struggle, an' never to cringe or fall—
Still I worked for Charley, for Charley was now my all;
And Charley was pretty good to me, with scarce a word or
frown,
Till at last he went a-courtin', and brought a wife from town.

She was somewhat dressy, an' hadn't a pleasant smile—
She was quite conceity, and carried a heap o' style;
But if ever I tried to be friends, I did with her, I know;
But she was hard and proud, an' I couldn't make it go.

She had an edication, an' that was good for her;
But when she twitted me on mine, 'twas carryin' things too
fur;
An' I told her once, 'fore company (an' it almost made her
sick),
That I never swallowed a grammar, or 'et a 'rithmetic.

So 'twas only a few days before the thing was done—
They was a family of themselves, and I another one;
And a very little cottage one family will do,
But I never have seen a house that was big enough for two.

An' I never could speak to suit her, never could please her eye,
An' it made me independent, an' then I didn't try;
But I was terribly staggered, an' felt it like a blow,
When Charley turned ag'in me, an' told me I could go.

I went to live with Susan, but Susan's house was small,
And she was always a-hintin' how snug it was for us all;
And what with her husband's sisters, and what with child'rn
three,
'Twas easy to discover that there wasn't room for me.

An' then I went to Thomas, the oldest son I've got,
For Thomas's buildings 'd cover the half of an acre lot;
But all the child'rn was on me—I couldn't stand their sauce—
And Thomas said I needn't think I was comin' there to boss.

An' then I wrote to Rebecca, my girl who lives out West,
And to Isaac, not far from her—some twenty miles at best;
And one of 'em said 'twas too warm there for any one so old,
And t'other had an opinion the climate was too cold.

So they have shirked and slighted me, an' shifted me about—
So they have well-nigh soured me, an' wore my old heart out;
But still I've borne up pretty well, an' wasn't much put down,
Till Charley went to the poor-master, an' put me on the town.

Over the hill to the poor-house—my child'rn dear, good-by!
Many a night I've watched you when only God was nigh;
And God 'll judge between us; but I will al'ays pray
That you shall never suffer the half I do to-day.

Over the Hill from the Poor-House

Over the hill to the poor-house *I* went, one winter's day:
I—who was always considered a "bad stick" anyway;
I—who was always gettin' in a large assortment of tricks,
And always sure to be quoted as "the worst of the Deacon's
 six."

Tom was a steady fellow, and saved up all he got;
But when it came to payin' his debts, he'd always rather not;
And Isaac could quote the Scriptures, an' never forgot nor
 slipped;
But "Honor thy father and mother" was one of the verses he
 skipped.

An' as for Susan an' 'Becca, their hearts, as one might say,
Was good—what there was of 'em—which wasn't much, any-
 way;
And all of our little family was good as you'll often see,
Exceptin' one poor fellow—and that 'ere one was me.

All of the rest was steady, an' nice, an' good, an' right;
All of the rest was sober—but I was mainly tight;

An' when I "borrowed" two horses, or helped to, just for
 fun—
If I hadn't been drunk as blazes, it never would have been
 done.

But when they sent me to prison, the hardest grief I felt
Was when my poor old mother beside me feebly knelt,
And cried and prayed all round me, till I got melted down,
And cried as I wouldn't have cried that day for half the horses
 in town.

And with my left arm round her—my right hand lifted high—
I swore henceforth to be honest, and sober live and die;
And I went and served my term out, although 'twas a bitter pill,
Which many fellows ought to take who probably never will.

And when I had served my sentence, I thought 'twould answer
 the best
To take the advice of Greeley: "Go West, young man, go
 West!"
And how I came to prosper there, I never could understand;
But Fortune seemed to like me—she gave me a winning
 hand!

And year after year I prospered, and kept a-going ahead;
And wrote to a trusty neighbor East, to tell 'em that I was
 dead;
And died a good straight fellow; for I knew it would please
 them more
Than if I had lived to a hundred and twelve—the chap that I
 was before!

But when this trusty neighbor—he wrote a line to me—
"Your mother's in the poor-house, a-pining away," says he,
To keep dead any longer—I knew that it wouldn't be right;
So I'd a private resurrection, and started for her that night.

And when I came in the old town, my first act was to buy
A snug and handsome cottage, which rather seemed to my eye
To look just like the old one; I finished it off the same;
You couldn't have told the difference—if you could, *I* wasn't
 to blame!

The same old clock in the corner; the fireplace, wide and
 high,
Sent up the smoke and cinders, and flung them towards the
 sky;

From garret down to cellar—'twas all the self-same thing:
'Twas good enough for the President—'twas fine enough for
 a king!

Then over the hill to the poor-house, one blustering winter day,
With two fleet nags and a cutter, I swiftly took my way:
The fleetest nags in the county, and both as black as coal—
They very much resembled the pair of horses I stole.

I hitched in front of the poor-house—I opened the poor-
 house door;
My poor old mother was on her knees, a-scrubbin' the kitchen
 floor!
I coughed a little, on purpose—she started, in surprise—
Rose up, with a scared expression, an' looked me in the eyes.

I slowly walked up to her, an' all her troubles' trace
I saw in the lines of sorrow that marred her dear old face:
"Mother, O Mother!" I shouted; "your poor-house contract's
 done;
An' you henceforth are adopted, by your resurrected son!"

She didn't faint nor holloa—but knelt down by my side,
And thanked the Lord for saving her me, till I broke down and
 cried;
But maybe our ride wasn't merry! and maybe we wasn't gay!
And maybe I didn't wrap her up that blustering winter day!

And maybe, when we had got home, and entered the cottage
 door,
She didn't start back kind of sudden—as if she'd seen it
 before!
And maybe it wasn't pleasant—our cosey evening tea—
With her quite often stoppin', and huggin' and kissin' me!

And maybe we didn't live happy, for quite a number of years!
And I gained the respect of my neighbors—in spite of my
 brothers' sneers,
And spite of my sisters' caution; who said, as I have heard,
That they never could own a brother that had been a prison
 bird!

But I'll bet, when the great bugle rings out its cheerful notes,
And the good Lord Almighty sorts out His sheep and goats,
However my case is settled, if you are there you'll see
That my old Christian mother will stand right up for me.

JULIA A. (FLETCHER) CARNEY
(1823–1908)

I OWN A yellowed clipping from an unidentified Boston newspaper that is a lengthy obituary of Julia Carney. She was born in Lancaster, Massachusetts. When she was 22, and teaching a primary grade in Boston, she enrolled in a shorthand class. Asked to write a bit of verse in shorthand, she jotted down the first stanza of "Little Things." When a Universalist church Sunday School paper, the *Gospel Teacher* (later the *Myrtle*), asked for a contribution, she added three more stanzas. No date for this publication is given.

Merle Johnson, in *You Know These Lines!* (1935), has a seemingly different account. He quotes from a letter Carney sent to the Boston *Transcript* saying "the poem first appeared in an eight-page leaflet," published by J. M. Usher of Boston. Was this leaflet the *Gospel Teacher?* In any case, the poem was soon appearing in newspapers all over the land, usually with no byline.

The poem was soon set to music, working its way into countless hymnals and anthologies where it was falsely credited to Reverend Ebenezer Cobham Brewer. Brewer was a prolific British author best known today for his *Reader's Handbook* and his *Dictionary of Phrase and Fable*. A German woman had asked him for a copy of the poem. He responded that he did not know who the author was, and that he had added a fifth stanza of his own. I found this stanza in Roger Ingpen's 1903 collection *One Thousand Poems for Children,* where the poem is credited to Dr. Brewer:

> Little seeds of mercy,
> Sown by youthful hands,
> Grow to bless the nations
> Far in heathen lands.

As late as 1946, when Elizabeth Hough Schrist based her *One Thousand Poems for Children* on Ingpen's earlier anthology, the poem was still credited to Brewer and had his added final stanza.

The next to last line of the original poem was, "Make this pleasant earth below." When the poem appeared as a singing exercise in a school textbook, it was changed to "Make our earth an Eden." Carney did not like this, so she altered the line to its present "Help to make earth happy."

Carney's husband was a Universalist minister who pastored churches in many different U. S. cities, including Chicago and Beloit, Wisconsin. After he died in 1871, Carney settled in Holyoke, Massachusetts.

I know of no book by this poet. Of her many other deeply spiritual poems, the one appearing most often in hymn books of the time was "Think Gently of the Erring." It is hard to find two versions exactly alike. The one here is from an undated London book titled *Christian Lyrics*. The poem has no byline, nor does the book name its compiler.

Little Things

Little drops of water,
 Little grains of sand,
Make the mighty ocean
 And the pleasant land.

So the little moments,
 Humble though they be,
Make the mighty ages
 Of eternity.

So our little errors
 Lead the soul away
From the path of virtue,
 Far in sin to stray.

Little deeds of kindness,
 Little words of love,
Help to make earth happy
 Like the heaven above.

Think Gently of the Erring

Think gently of the erring:
 Ye know not of the power
With which the dark temptation came
 In some unguarded hour.
Ye may not know how earnestly
 They struggled, or how well,
Until the hour of weakness came
 And sadly thus they fell.

Think gently of the erring:
 Oh! do not thou forget,
However darkly stained by sin,
 He is thy brother yet;
Heir of the selfsame heritage,
 Child of the selfsame God,
He has but stumbled in the path
 Thou hast in weakness trod.

Speak gently to the erring:
 For is it not enough

That innocence and peace have gone,
 Without thy censure rough?
It sure must be a weary lot,
 That sin-stained heart to bear,
And those who share a happier fate
 Their chidings well may spare.

Speak gently to the erring:
 Thou yet may'st lead them back
With holy words and tones of love,
 From misery's thorny track:
Forget not thou hast often sinned,
 And sinful yet must be;
Deal gently with the erring, then,
 As God has dealt with thee.

WILLIAM HERBERT CARRUTH
(1859–1924)

ALL INFORMED theists today take for granted that evolution is God's technique
for creating the cosmos and the life we know. Carruth, who was born the same
year Darwin's *Origin of Species* was published, gave this assumption an eloquent
expression in the first stanza of his one famous poem.

Carruth was born at Osawatomie, Kansas, and obtained a Harvard Ph.D. in
1893. He taught modern languages and German literature at the University of
Kansas, where he was vice-president from 1887 until 1913. In 1913 he became
a professor of comparative literature at Stanford University.

"Each in His Own Tongue" was first published in 1906, though I don't know
where. It was included in *Each in His Own Tongue and Other Poems* (1908). I own
a small book printing of the poem, illustrated in color by an unnamed artist,
and published by Wise-Penslow, New York. There is no date, but the title page
has a note saying the book was copyrighted in 1925 by P. F. Volland, suggesting
an earlier edition.

Each in His Own Tongue

A fire-mist and a planet,
 A crystal and a cell,
A jelly-fish and a saurian,
 And caves where the cave-men dwell;
Then a sense of law and beauty
 And a face turned from the clod—

Some call it Evolution,
 And others call it God.

A haze on the far horizon,
 The infinite, tender sky,
The ripe rich tint of the cornfields,
 And the wild geese sailing high—
And all over upland and lowland
 The charm of the golden-rod—
Some of us call it Autumn
 And others call it God.

Like tides on a crescent sea-beach,
 When the moon is new and thin,
Into our hearts high yearnings
 Come welling and surging in—
Come from the mystic ocean,
 Whose rim no foot has trod,—
Some of us call it Longing,
 And others call it God.

A picket frozen on duty,
 A mother starved for her brood,
Socrates drinking the hemlock,
 And Jesus on the rood;
And millions who, humble and nameless,
 The straight, hard pathway plod,—
Some call it Consecration,
 And others call it God.

PHILA HENRIETTA CASE
(?–?)

ACCORDING TO *The Star Speaker* (1894 edition), edited by Flora Kightlinger, this poem was first published in *Schoolday Magazine* (March 1867), and set to music in 1892 by "E. D." The poem appears in dozens of nineteenth-century anthologies, usually without credit or wrongly attributed to Phila H. Child. The poem could be written today about runaway teenaged girls who find themselves starving on big city streets.

 Who was Phila Case? Did she write other poems? When and where did she live and die? The author of this once famous poem seems to have become "nobody's poet."

Nobody's Child

Alone in the dreary, pitiless street,
With my torn old dress, and bare, cold feet,
All day I have wandered to and fro,
Hungry and shivering, and nowhere to go;
The night's coming on in darkness and dread,
And the chill sleet beating upon my bare head.
Oh! why does the wind blow upon me so wild?
Is it because I am nobody's child?

Just over the way there's a flood of light,
And warmth and beauty, and all things bright;
Beautiful children, in robes so fair,
Are carolling songs in their rapture there.
I wonder if they, in their blissful glee,
Would pity a poor little beggar like me,
Wandering alone in the merciless street,
Naked and shivering, and nothing to eat?

Oh! what shall I do when the night comes down,
In its terrible blackness all over the town?
Shall I lay me down 'neath the angry sky,
On the cold, hard pavement, alone to die,
When the beautiful children their prayers have said,
And their mammas have tucked them up snugly in bed?
For no dear mother on *me* ever smiled,—
Why is it, I wonder, I'm nobody's child?

No father, no mother, no sister, not one
In all the world loves me, e'en the little dogs run
When I wander too near them; 'tis wondrous to see,
How everything shrinks from a beggar like me!
Perhaps 'tis a dream; but sometimes, when I lie
Gazing far up in the dark blue sky,
Watching for hours, some large, bright star,
I fancy the beautiful gates are ajar,

And a host of white-robed nameless things,
Come fluttering o'er me on gilded wings;
A hand that is strangely soft and fair
Caresses gently my tangled hair,
And a voice like the carol of some wild bird—
The sweetest voice that was ever heard—

Calls me many a dear, pet name,
Till my heart and spirit are all aflame.

They tell me of such unbounded love,
And bid me come up to their home above;
And then with such pitiful, sad surprise,
They look at me with their sweet, tender eyes,
And it seems to me, out of the dreary night,
I am going up to that world of light;
And away from the hunger and storm so wild,
I am sure I shall then be somebody's child.

RUTH CHESTERFIELD
(?–?)

"THE GRUMBLING OLD WOMAN" is anonymous in all old collections of verse I have seen except Flora Kightlinger's *The Star Speaker* (n.d.) where it is credited to Ruth Chesterfield. John Foster Kirk's *Supplement to Allibone's Dictionary of Authors* (1891) has only this after her name: "New Version of Old Mother Hubbard, Boston, 1866." I don't know if this refers to the poem or to a book containing the poem.

The Grumbling Old Woman

There was an old woman, and—what do you think?—
She lived upon nothing but victuals and drink!
But though victuals and drink were the chief of her diet,
Yet this grumbling old woman never was quiet.

She had a nice cottage, a hen-house and barn,
And a sheep whose fine wool furnished blankets and yarn;
A cow that supplied her with butter and cheese,
A large flock of geese, and a hive full of bees.

Yet she grumbled and grumbled from morning till night,
For this foolish old woman thought nothing went right;
E'en the days of the week were all wrong, for on Sunday
She always declared that she wished it was Monday.

If cloudless and fair was the long summer day,
And the sun smiled down on the new-mown hay,
"There's a drouth," she said, "as sure as you're born!
If it doesn't rain soon, it will ruin the corn!"

But when descended the gentle rain,
Blessing the bountiful fields of grain,
And bringing new life to flower and bud,
She said there was coming a second flood.

She never gave aught to the needy and poor;
The outcast and hungry she turned from her door.
"Shall I work," she said, with a wag of the head,
"To provide for the idle and lazy their bread?"

But the rich she regarded with envy and spite;
She said 'twas a shame,—'twasn't decent nor right,—
That the haughty old squire, with his bow-legged son,
Should ride with two horses, while she rode with one.

And the crabbed old fellow—to spite her, no doubt,—
Had built a new barn like a palace throughout,
With a cupola on it, as grand as you please,
And a rooster that whirled head and tail with the breeze.

"I wish, so I do," she said, cocking her eye,
"There'd come a great whirlwind, and blow it sky-high!"
And e'en as she spoke, a loud rushing was heard,
And the barn to its very foundations was stirred.

It stood the shock bravely, but—pitiful sight!—
The wind took the old woman up like a kite!
As she sailed up aloft over forest and hill,
Her tongue, so they say, it kept wagging on still.

And where she alighted, no mortal doth know,
Or whether she ever alighted below.

MORAL.

My moral, my dears, you will find if you try;
And if you don't find any, neither can I.

LYDIA MARIA (FRANCIS) CHILD
(1802–1880)

LYDIA MARIA CHILD was one of the nation's most prolific nineteenth-century writers, as well as one of its most influential abolitionists. She was also an energetic advocate for women's rights and the rights of Native Americans. She produced a two-volume *History of the Condition of Women in Various Ages and*

Nations (1835). Another two-volume tome, *An Appeal in Favor of that Class of Americans called Africans* (1833), was the first book to detail the horrors of our country's system of slavery. It created a sensation. In addition she wrote several historical novels (in one of them, *Philothea* [1836], Plato is a character), short stories, essays, biographies, histories and verse.

Born in Medford, Massachusetts, "Miss Francis" began her career as a private school teacher in Watertown. In 1826 she founded and for nine years edited the bimonthly *Juvenile Miscellany,* America's first significant magazine for children. Sarah Josepha Hale's poem about Mary's little lamb first appeared in this magazine. Hale followed Child as editor, and later became editor of *Godey's Lady's Book.* It was she who persuaded Abraham Lincoln to make Thanksgiving a national holiday.

In 1841 Child and her attorney husband David Lee Child moved to New York City to edit for four years the weekly *Anti-Slavery Standard.* Her colorful sketches of city life appeared in two volumes of *Letters from New York. Process of Religious Ideas through Successive Ages,* in three volumes, was her most ambitious work. She also found time to write one of the earliest books on home economics, *The Frugal Housewife* (1829; it had thirty-five editions), and a pioneering cookbook, *The Mother's Book* (1831). The poet Whittier wrote a biographical introduction to a posthumous collection of her letters (1882) in which he called her a "wise and brave, but tender and loving woman." His poem "Within the Gate" is a seventeen-stanza elegy on her death.

In almost all anthologies, "Thanksgiving Day" is severely truncated. Here you will find (thanks to Dr. Joseph Valeriani, of the Medford Historical Society) all twelve original stanzas. They first appeared in the second volume of Child's *Flowers for Children* (1844); I do not know who first set it to a French folk tune. "Grandmother's House" is sometimes substituted throughout for "grandfather's house," but as Dr. Valeriani points out, grandmother is not mentioned until the next to last stanza.

A short story by John O'Hara, "Over the River and Through the Wood," takes its title from the first line of Child's poem. In 1964 he included it in a book called *The Horse Knows the Way,* the third line of the same stanza.

With the exception of Child's history of world religions, all her books mentioned here are currently in print, as well as a few of her other works. "Over the River and Through the Wood," glowingly illustrated in color by Brinton Turkle, was published by Coward, McCann in 1974. It contains all twelve stanzas with spellings and punctuation slightly updated.

The old wooden drawbridge over the Mystic River in Medford has long been replaced by a granite and concrete one, and where Child's ancestral home once stood, at the corner of Salem and Ashland, there is now a Chinese restaurant. About a mile away was the home of James S. Pierpont, who wrote the words and music of "Jingle Bells."

Thanksgiving Day

Over the river, and through the wood,
 To grandfather's house we go;
The horse knows the way,
 To carry the sleigh,
Through the white and drifted snow.

Over the river, and through the wood,
 To grandfather's house away!
We would not stop
 For doll or top,
For 'tis Thanksgiving day.

Over the river, and through the wood,
 Oh, how the wind does blow!
It stings the toes
 And bites the nose,
As over the ground we go.

Over the river, and through the wood,
 With a clear blue winter sky,
The dogs do bark
 And children hark,
As we go jingling by.

Over the river, and through the wood,
 To have a first-rate-play—
Hear the bells ring
 Ting a ling ding,
Hurra for Thanksgiving day!

Over the river, and through the wood—
 No matter for winds that blow;
Or if we get
 The sleigh upset,
Into a bank of snow.

Over the river, and through the wood,
 To see little John and Ann;
We will kiss them all,
 And play snow-ball,
And stay as long as we can.

Over the river, and through the wood,
 Trot fast, my dapple gray!

Spring over the ground,
 Like a hunting hound,
For 'tis Thanksgiving day!

Over the river, and through the wood,
 And straight through the barn-yard gate
We seem to go
 Extremely slow,
It is so hard to wait.

Over the river, and through the wood—
 Old Jowler hears our bells;
He shakes his paw
 With a loud bow wow,
And thus the news he tells.

Over the river, and through the wood—
 When grandmother sees us come,
She will say, Oh dear
 The children are here,
Bring a pie for every one.

Over the river, and through the wood—
 Now grandmother's cap I spy!
Hurra for the fun!
 Is the pudding done?
Hurra for the pumpkin pie!

SARAH NORCLIFFE CLEGHORN
(1876–1959)

SARAH CLEGHORN was a democratic socialist who wrote vast quantities of verse for U.S. magazines. Born in Norfolk, Virginia, she spent most of her life in Manchester, Vermont. At age 35 she became active in the Socialist Party of Eugene Debs and Norman Thomas. For the remainder of her life she was an ardent pacifist, worker for prison reform and vigorous opponent of child labor and vivisection.

Cleghorn, who never married, divided her verse into what she called her "sunbonnet" poems about country life, and her "burning" poems of social protest. They were much admired by her fellow Vermont poet Robert Frost. Many of her poems, such as "Ballad of Gene Debs," were first issued as pamphlets. She also wrote a novel, *The Spinster* (1916), and coauthored a novel (*Fellow Captains*, 1916) and a play (*Understand Betsy*) with Dorothy Canfield Fisher. Her 1936 autobiography, *Threescore*, was reprinted by Ayer in 1980.

All of Cleghorn's poetry has vanished into oblivion except for "The Golf Links." Only four lines long, it ranks with Elizabeth Barrett Browning's "Cry of the Children" as one of the most effective verse attacks on child labor. I am told that it first appeared in 1915 in Franklin P. Adams's newspaper column, and later in Cleghorn's collection of poems, *Portraits and Protests* (1917). Her *Poems of Peace and Freedom* was published in 1945.

It is difficult to believe, but "The Golf Links," a passionate protest against child labor, turns up in several anthologies of light and humorous verse.

The Golf Links

The golf links lie so near the mill
 That almost every day
The laboring children can look out
 And see the men at play.

EDMUND VANCE COOKE
(1866–1932)

ALL I COULD learn about Cooke was from a brief entry in *Who Was Who in America*. He was born in Port Denver, Canada, but settled in Cleveland, where he died. A dozen books of his verse are listed.

"How Did You Die?" is from *Impertinent Poems* (1903) but surely was published earlier in a newspaper or magazine. Another of his popular poems, found in anthologies, is "Rags," a heart-rending account of a faithful dog who gets lost and ends up on a vivisection table. Who should be carving him open but the dog's previous owner, now studying medicine! Rags recognizes him, wags his tail, licks the young medic's hands and dies. The last two stanzas are:

> Well! I've seen men go to courageous death
> In the air, on sea, and land!
> But only a dog would spend his breath
> In a kiss for his murderer's hand.
>
> And if there's no heaven for love like that,
> For such four-legged fealty—well!
> If I have any choice, I tell you flat,
> I'll take my chance in hell.

How Did You Die?

Did you tackle that trouble that came your way
 With a resolute heart and cheerful?
Or hide your face from the light of day
 With a craven soul and fearful?
Oh, a trouble's a ton, or a trouble's an ounce,
 Or a trouble is what you make it.
And it isn't the fact that you're hurt that counts,
 But only how did you take it?

You are beaten to earth? Well, well, what's that?
 Come up with a smiling face.
It's nothing against you to fall down flat,
 But to lie there—that's disgrace.
The harder you're thrown, why the higher you bounce;
 Be proud of your blackened eye!
It isn't the fact that you're licked that counts;
 It's how did you fight and why?

And though you be done to death, what then?
 If you battled the best you could;
If you played your part in the world of men,
 Why, the Critic will call it good.
Death comes with a crawl, or comes with a pounce,
 And whether he's slow or spry,
It isn't the fact that you're dead that counts,
 But only, how did you die?

HUGH ANTOINE D'ARCY
(1843–1925)

I KNOW NOTHING about d'Arcy's life except the dates of his birth and death, and I'm not even sure of those.

"The Face Upon the Floor," usually titled "The Face on the Barroom Floor," is said to have first appeared in the New York *Dispatch* in 1887. In 1890 a small book of poems by d'Arcy was published in Brooklyn, titled *The Face Upon the Floor and Other Ballads*. The author states in a short preface to a later edition (1912) that he wrote the poem in 1887, and was astonished by how quickly it caught on. It was a favorite recitation of Maurice Barrymore, father of Ethel, John and Lionel. The first speaker's anthology to include it was probably *Standard Recitations* (New York, 1889).

Among several false claimants, one John Henry Titus made the most racket. He insisted he wrote the poem as a boy in Jefferson, Ohio, and that it appeared in the Jefferson *Sentinel* in 1872, although he never supplied the exact date or produced a copy. His version of the poem is so markedly inferior that there is no doubt he wrote it after d'Arcy's poem appeared. Titus also claimed he wrote the post office motto about rain, snow and sleet—a translation of a sentence by Herodotus.

The reference to the *sou* in the fourth stanza suggests that the painter came from France, but stanza ten says he sold a painting for fifteen hundred pounds, implying a life in England. His English residence is strengthened by the twelfth stanza, in which he likens Madeleine's eyes to the Koh-i-noor—a famous diamond from India with a violent history. Since 1849 it has been one of England's crown jewels.

Joseph Morris and St. Clair Adams, in their anthology *The Light of the World* (1928), introduce d'Arcy's poem with an account of its origin that may or may not be true. D'Arcy, they say, was a "theatrical man" who one Saturday night was having a drink in a Union Square bar, in Manhattan. A bum who entered the bar was tossed out on the street. D'Arcy left the bar to give the man a drink and some money, and when asked what he did for a living, the man replied that he was an artist. Angry, d'Arcy went home and wrote his poem "as an admonition to all to be kind to the poor derelict."

Although d'Arcy's ballad has nothing to do with the dangers of strong drink, the temperance movement seized on the poem and distributed it far and wide. In 1925 d'Arcy said: "If I thought my poem had done anything to help Prohibition, I would go take a running jump into the Hudson."

In 1936 Herndon Davis, a well-known illustrator for the *Denver Post,* painted Madeleine's face on the wooden floor of a bar in the Teller House Casino, Central City, Colorado. As historians of the area tell it, an itinerant actor periodically came into the bar to recite d'Arcy's ballad, then pass the hat. As a joke, Davis slipped into the bar one night and painted on the floor the face of his wife Juanita. Part of the joke was the fact that Juanita was a dedicated prohibitionist. Davis covered the painting with a drop cloth. The next time the actor reached the climax of his recitation, Davis yanked away the cloth.

Since then "Madeleine"'s portrait, protected by surrounding posts in what is called the casino's Face Bar, has become one of the main attractions of this famous, opulent gambling casino (see frontispiece). Central City, in Clear Creek Canyon west of Denver, is one of Colorado's legendary gold mining "ghost towns." Every summer the Central City Opera performs "The Face on the Barroom Floor," a cabaret musical inspired by the poem and by Davis's haunting picture.

Hayward Cirker called my attention to echoes of d'Arcy's ballad in the song "One For My Baby (And One More For the Road)"—a song popularized by Frank Sinatra, who recorded it at least three times. Bartender Joe is mentioned in the song, and d'Arcy's line "Fill her up, Joe" becomes "Set 'em up, Joe," as the singer bemoans a lost love. The lyrics were written by Johnny Mercer, with music by Harold Arlen, to be sung by Fred Astaire in the 1943 film *The Sky's the Limit.*

Allow me to digress. A native of Savannah, Georgia, Johnny Mercer was one of America's greatest songwriters. Here are a few among hundreds of well-

known Mercer lyrics: "Ac-cent-tchu-ate the Positive," "And the Angels Sing," "Autumn Leaves," "Barefoot in the Park," "Blues in the Night," "Come Rain or Come Shine," "Days of Wine and Roses," "I'm an Old Cowhand," "In the Cool, Cool, Cool of the Evening," "Jeepers, Creepers," "Laura," "Lazybones," "Moon River," "On the Atchison, Topeka and the Santa Fe," "Tangerine," "That Old Black Magic" and "You Must Have Been a Beautiful Baby." Although unable to read music, Mercer also composed the tunes for many popular songs, and was a featured vocalist with Paul Whiteman's band and on Benny Goodman's radio show. In 1942 he founded Capitol Records. Although many of Mercer's and other songwriters' lyrics have poetic content, you won't find them in any anthologies—a convention that unfortunately excludes much good poetry. (I consider Mercer a better poet and a better man than Ezra Pound.)

The Face on the Barroom Floor

'Twas a balmy summer evening, and a goodly crowd was there,
Which well-nigh filled Joe's barroom on the corner of the square;
And as songs and witty stories came through the open door
A vagabond crept slowly in and posed upon the floor.

"Where did it come from?" some one said. "The wind has blown it in."
"What does it want?" another cried. "Some whiskey, rum or gin."
"Here, Toby, seek him if your stomach's equal to the work—
I wouldn't touch him with a fork, he's as filthy as a Turk."

This badinage the poor wretch took with stoical good grace;
In fact he smiled, as though he thought he'd struck the proper place.
"Come, boys, I know there's burly hearts among so good a crowd,
To be in such good company would make a deacon proud.

"Give me a drink—that's what I want—I'm out of funds you know,
When I had cash to treat the gang this hand was never slow.
What? You laugh as though you thought this pocket never held a sou!
I once was fixed as well, my boys, as any one of you.

"There, thanks! that's braced me nicely! God bless you one and all!
Next time I pass this good saloon I'll make another call.

Give you a song? No, I can't do that; my singing days are past;
My voice is cracked, my throat's worn out, and my lungs are
 going fast.

"Say! give me another whiskey, and I tell you what I'll do—
I'll tell you a funny story, and a fact, I promise, too.
That I was ever a decent man not one of you would think;
But I was, some four or five years back. Say, give me another
 drink.

"Fill her up, Joe; I want to put some life into my frame—
Such little drinks to a bum like me are miserably tame;
Five fingers—there, that's the scheme—and corking whiskey,
 too!
Well, here's luck, boys! and, landlord, my best regards to you!

"You've treated me pretty kindly, and I'd like to tell you how
I came to be the dirty sot you see before you now.
As I told you, once I was a man, with muscle, frame and
 health,
And but for a blunder ought to have made considerable
 wealth.

"I was a painter—not one that daubs on bricks and wood,
But an artist, and for my age was rated pretty good.
I worked hard at my canvas, and was bidding fair to rise,
For gradually I saw the star of fame before my eyes.

"I made a picture perhaps you've seen, 'tis called 'The Chase
 of Fame'?
It brought me fifteen hundred pounds and added to my
 name.
And then I met a woman—now comes the funny part—
With eyes that petrified my brain and sunk into my heart.

"Why don't you laugh? 'Tis funny that the vagabond you see
Could ever love a woman and expect her love for me;
But 'twas so, and for a month or two her smiles were freely
 given,
And when her lovely lips touched mine it carried me to
 heaven.

"Did you ever see a woman for whom your soul you'd give,
With a form like the Milo Venus, too beautiful to live;
With eyes that would beat the Koh-i-noor, and a wealth of
 chestnut hair?
If so, 'twas she, for there never was another half so fair.

"I was working on a portrait, one afternoon in May,
Of a fair-haired boy, a friend of mine, who lived across the way;
And Madeleine admired it, and, much to my surprise,
Said that she'd like to know the man that had such dreamy
 eyes.

"It didn't take long to know him, and before the month had
 flown
My friend had stolen my darling, and I was left alone;
And ere a year of misery had passed above my head
The jewel I had treasured so had tarnished, and was dead!

"That's why I took to drink, boys. Why, I never saw you smile!
I thought you'd be amused, and laughing all the while.
Why, what's the matter, friend? There's a teardrop in your eye!
Come, laugh, like me; 'tis only babes and women that should
 cry.

"Say, boys! if you give me just another whiskey I'll be glad,
And I'll draw right here a picture of the face that drove me
 mad.
Give me that piece of chalk with which you mark the baseball
 score,
You shall see the lovely Madeleine upon the barroom floor."

Another drink, and with chalk in hand the vagabond began
To sketch a face that well might buy the soul of any man;
Then as he placed another lock upon the shapely head,
With a fearful shriek he leaped and fell across the picture—
 dead.

MARIE RAVENAL DE LA COSTE
(?–?)

THIS SENTIMENTAL doggerel about a dying soldier appears in many nineteenth-century anthologies. William Cullen Bryant in his massive *Library of Poetry and Song*, attributes it to anonymous. Other collections of verse spell De La Coste's last name as "Caste." All I could find out about her is the following paragraph in an undated anthology titled *What Can a Woman Do, or Her Position in the Business and Literary World*, edited by Mrs. M. L. Rayne:

> This exquisite ballad is usually published as anonymous. Like Beautiful Snow, it has had a number of claimants, but no name has remained attached to it until Epes Sargent rescued it in 1880, and published it in his collection, with extracts from letters written by

Miss La Caste. The poem was first published, with her name attached, in the Southern Churchman. She was living in Savannah, Georgia, when she published it. She is of French parentage, and dislikes anything like notoriety. She is an attractive lady, accomplished, and of superior mental qualifications, but has no desire to shine in the world of letters.

I have been unable to check Sargent's anthology, *Harper's Encyclopedia of British and American Poetry* (1881). On Sargent, see his poem "A Life on the Ocean Wave," included in this volume. I have copied the poem from Bryant's collection.

Somebody's Darling

Into a ward of the whitewashed walls
 Where the dead and the dying lay—
Wounded by bayonets, shells, and balls—
 Somebody's darling was borne one day.
Somebody's darling! so young and so brave,
 Wearing still on his pale, sweet face—
Soon to be hid by the dust of the grave—
 The lingering light of his boyhood's grace.

Matted and damp are the curls of gold,
 Kissing the snow of that fair young brow;
Pale are the lips of delicate mould—
 Somebody's darling is dying now.
Back from the beautiful blue-veined face
 Brush every wandering, silken thread;
Cross his hands as a sign of grace—
 Somebody's darling is still and dead!

Kiss him once for Somebody's sake;
 Murmur a prayer, soft and low;
One bright curl from the cluster take—
 They were Somebody's pride, you know.
Somebody's hand hath rested there;
 Was it a mother's, soft and white?
And have the lips of a sister fair
 Been baptized in those waves of light?

God knows best. He was Somebody's love?
 Somebody's heart enshrined him here;
 Somebody wafted his name above,
 Night and morn, on the wings of prayer.

Somebody wept when he marched away,
 Looking so handsome, brave, and grand;
Somebody's kiss on his forehead lay;
 Somebody clung to his parting hand—

Somebody's watching and waiting for him,
 Yearning to hold him again to her heart:
There he lies—with the blue eyes dim,
 And smiling, child-like lips apart.
Tenderly bury the fair young dead,
 Pausing to drop on his grave a tear,
Carve on the wooden slab at his head,
 "Somebody's darling lies buried here!"

SARAH DOUDNEY
(1843–1926)

"THE LESSON OF THE WATER-MILL," widely reprinted in America and England from 1870 to 1900, was a favorite of professional reciters. It is still found in anthologies of popular verse. The author, Sarah Doudney, was a London writer who first published her famous poem in 1864 in *The Children's Family Magazine,* and later in her volume of poetry *Psalms of Life* (1871).

In 1870 Scottish-born Daniel Craig McCallum (1815–1875) privately published in Brooklyn a book titled *The Water-Mill and Other Poems.* It included Doudney's poem, slightly altered for the worse, with an added stanza as dreadful as all the other poems in the book. McCallum was an Erie Railway superintendent living in Oswego, New York, who had served for the North in the Civil War as a major-general. Perhaps he thought "The Water-Mill" was his own work because he had tinkered with it.

I was amazed to discover how completely Doudney has vanished from reference books on British writers. You won't find her in *The Oxford Companion to English Literature,* or in *British Authors of the Nineteenth Century.* Yet in the *Supplement to Alibone's Critical Dictionary of English Literature* (1891) there is a long entry listing forty-one of her books, including novels, short stories and verse. As she was then still living, no doubt her final bibliography is even longer. I know nothing about the water-mills of her life.

I own an old undated scrapbook in which are pasted down poems that appeared in a newspaper called *The Globe,* for a series titled "Poems You Ought to Know." Accompanying "The Lesson of the Water-Mill" is a letter Doudney sent to *The Globe* telling how she wrote the poem:

> I wrote "The Lesson of the Water-Mill" when I was about 16. One day I was sitting in a bay-window, overlooking a road in Portsmouth, and turning the pages of a scrapbook to amuse a child. Suddenly I came upon a picture of a water-mill, and under the engraving was the

proverb, "The mill cannot grind with the water that is past." I had never seen a water-mill. My birthplace was near the sea and I knew very little of river scenery. But when the child had gone away and I was left alone, I thought about the picture and the proverb. And so the song was written, singing itself into my head, as all my songs have done. While I copy the lines for the *Globe* my thoughts go back to the days when they were written, and I call up a vision of my mother's face, bright with sympathy, when she heard my verses. Now I am left alone, living very near my birthplace, on the road which leads from Portsmouth to London. The poem first appeared in the *Churchman's Family Magazine*. Many years ago, long after the publication of the poem, Mr. Irving Bishop, the thought reader, visited London and saw the lines in my collection of verses, *Psalms of Life*. He had already bought the copyright of the poem from Mr. McCallum, who claimed the authorship. I met Mr. Bishop and proved my own claim to his entire satisfaction.

Many anthologies of the 1880s reprinted Doudney's poem, falsely crediting it to McCallum. I will cite only two that I own: *The Beautiful, the Wonderful, and the Wise* (1883), edited by L. N. Chapin, and *Star of Progress* (1888), edited by H. W. Smith.

The Lesson of the Water-Mill

Listen to the water-mill;
 Through the livelong day,
How the clicking of its wheel
 Wears the hours away!
Languidly the autumn wind,
 Stirs the forest leaves,
From the field the reapers sing,
 Binding up their sheaves;
And a proverb haunts my mind
 As a spell is cast—
"The mill cannot grind
 With the water that is past."

Autumn winds revive no more
 Leaves that once are shed,
And the sickle cannot reap
 Corn once gatherèd;
Flows the ruffled streamlet on,
 Tranquil, deep, and still;
Never gliding back again
 To the water-mill;

Truly speaks the proverb old
 With a meaning vast—
"The mill cannot grind
 With the water that is past."

Take the lesson to thyself,
 True and loving heart;
Golden youth is fleeting by,
 Summer hours depart;
Learn to make the most of life,
 Lose no happy day;
Time will never bring thee back
 Chances swept away!
Leave no tender word unsaid,
 Love while love shall last—
"The mill cannot grind
 With the water that is past."

Work while yet the daylight shines,
 Man of strength and will!
Never does the streamlet glide
 Useless by the mill;
Wait not till to-morrow's sun
 Beams upon thy way,
All that thou canst call thine own
 Lies in thy "To-day";
Power, intellect and health
 May not always last—
"The mill cannot grind
 With the water that is past."

Oh, the wasted hours of life
 That have drifted by!
Oh, the good that might have been—
 Lost, without a sigh!
Love that we might once have saved
 By a single word,
Thoughts conceived, but never penned,
 Perishing unheard;—
Take the proverb to thine heart,
 Take, and hold it fast—
"The mill cannot grind
 With the water that is past."

THOMAS DUNN ENGLISH
(1819–1902)

WHEN I WAS a boy I thought "Ben Bolt" was about a woman with the curious name of Alice Ben Bolt, not knowing a comma separated Alice from Ben. I doubt if anyone sings the lyrics these days, though I once heard Isaac Asimov, who had a fine singing voice, belt out all the verses.

"Ben Bolt" was not written as a song, but as a poem. It appeared in the *New York Mirror* in September 1843. The author, Thomas English, was then only 24. Born in Philadelphia of Irish Quaker parents, he tried his hand at both medicine and law before settling on a career as writer and journalist. (His M.D. thesis at the University of Pennsylvania had been a defense of phrenology.)

In New York City he edited two failed periodicals, the *Aurora* and the *Aristidean*. Back in Philadelphia, his weekly humor magazine *John Donkey* also soon bit the dust. Turning to politics, he became the first mayor of Lawnsville (now Logan), Virginia, and later served on the New Jersey legislature. He was a Democratic member of Congress from 1891 to 1895.

English wrote several novels, and some fifty plays of which only one, *The Mormons; or, Life at Salt Lake* (1858), was published. *Select Poems of Dr. Thomas Dunn English* appeared in 1894. He and Edgar Allan Poe were at first friends, then turned bitter enemies when English accused Poe of forgery. "He is not alone thoroughly unprincipled, base and depraved," wrote English, "but silly, vain and ignorant—not alone an assassin in morals, but a quack in literature." Poe called him Thomas Done Brown. When Poe sued the New York *Evening Mirror*, in which English's remarks had appeared, he was awarded $225.06 in damages.

After Nelson Kneass set "Ben Bolt" to a German air, it became one of the most loved songs of America and England. "Maudlin sentimentality was the prevailing, the indispensable, note in the popular songs of that epoch," writes Burton E. Stevenson in a chapter on "Ben Bolt" in *Famous Single Poems*, "but 'Ben Bolt' outmaudlined the worst of them." Its popularity was fading when in 1894 it was revived by a prominent mention in George du Maurier's best-selling novel *Trilby. The Oxford Companion to English Literature* says it was set to music no less than 26 times, once by English himself. (If you listen closely, you can hear Vivien Leigh/Scarlett Butler sing, "Oh she wept with delight when he gave her a smile / And trembled with fear at his frown.")

It is one of the great ironies of literary history that all of English's novels, plays and poems are now totally forgotten except for what Stevenson calls the "metrical indiscretion of his youth." That, he adds, "was the awful fate which English had unthinkingly brought upon himself."

Many parodies of "Ben Bolt" were written. Here is the first stanza of "Joe Jones" that I found in *The Speaker's Garland*, 2, no. 7 (1874):

> Don't you remember lame Sally, Joe Jones—
> Lame Sally, whose nose was so brown?
> Who looked like a clam if you gave her a smile,
> And went into fits at your frown?

In the old goose-pond in the orchard, Joe Jones,
 Where the goslings are learning to swim,
Lame Sally went fishing one wet, windy day,
 And there by mistake tumbled in.

In a little booklet titled *Good Old-Time Songs, No. 4* (1916), I found two anonymous sequels to English's poem, both of which follow.

Ben Bolt

Don't you remember sweet Alice, Ben Bolt,—
 Sweet Alice whose hair was so brown,
Who wept with delight when you gave her a smile,
 And trembled with fear at your frown?

In the old churchyard in the valley, Ben Bolt,
 In a corner obscure and alone,
They have fitted a slab of the granite so gray,
 And Alice lies under the stone.

Under the hickory tree, Ben Bolt,
 Which stood at the foot of the hill,
Together we've lain in the noonday shade,
 And listened to Appleton's mill.

The mill-wheel has fallen to pieces, Ben Bolt,
 The rafters have tumbled in,
And a quiet which crawls round the walls as you gaze
 Has followed the olden din.

Do you mind of the cabin of logs, Ben Bolt,
 At the edge of the pathless wood,
And the button-ball tree[1] with its motley limbs,
 Which nigh by the doorstep stood?

The cabin to ruin has gone, Ben Bolt,
 The tree you would seek for in vain;
And where once the lords of the forest waved,
 Are grass and the golden grain.

And don't you remember the school, Ben Bolt,
 With the master so cruel and grim,
And the shaded nook in the running brook
 Where the children went to swim?

[1] *button-ball tree*] a tree in the plane-tree family, so called because of its small brown seed balls; also called buttonwood tree.

Grass grows on the master's grave, Ben Bolt,
 The spring of the brook is dry,
And of all the boys who were schoolmates then
 There are only you and I.

There is change in the things I loved, Ben Bolt,
 They have changed from the old to the new;
But I feel in the depths of my spirit the truth,
 There never was change in you.

Twelvemonths twenty have passed, Ben Bolt,
 Since first we were friends—yet I hail
Your presence a blessing, your friendship a truth,
 Ben Bolt of the salt-sea gale!

Ben Bolt's Reply (Anonymous)

Oh, yes, I remember her name with delight,
 Sweet Alice, so cherished and dear;
I seek her grave in the pale hour of night,
 And moisten the turf with a tear.
And when the heart is o'erburdened with woes
 I wander and muse all alone,
And long for the time when my heart shall repose
 Where sweet Alice lies, under the stone.

I roam through the woods where so joyous we've strayed,
 And recline on the green, sunny hill;
All things are bright in that beautiful glade,
 But my heart is all lonely and chill.
The hand that so fondly I pressed in my own,
 And the lips that were melting with love,
Are cold in the grave and I am left all alone,
 Till I meet with sweet Alice above.

Ah, well I remember the school-house and brook,
 And the master so kind and so true;
The wild, blooming flowers in the cool, shady nook,
 As fragrant with incense and dew;
But I weep not for thee, though so dear to my heart,
 Or the friends that have left me alone,
The bosom will heave, and the teardrop start,
 For sweet Alice lies under the stone.

Ben Bolt's Grave (Anonymous)

By the side of sweet Alice they have laid Ben Bolt,
 Where oft he longed to repose;
For there he would kneel with the early spring flowers,
 And plant on his darling the rose.

His heart was as true as the star to his gaze
 When tossed on the billows alone,
But now it is cold and forever at rest,
 For he calmly lies under the stone.

At last he is gone to the bright spirit lands,
 And free from all sorrow and pain;
He tastes the full rapture of angels above
 To meet with sweet Alice again.

We gather the flowers from the green, shady brook,
 And moss from the silent old mill,
To strew o'er the grave where now doth repose
 The hearts that death hardly could chill.

And oft when the soul has grown weary and sad
 We come by twilight alone
To muse o'er the spot where together Ben Bolt
 And sweet Alice lie under the stone.

JAMES THOMAS FIELDS
(1817–1881)

HAILING FROM Portsmouth, New Hampshire, Fields co-founded Ticknor and Fields, a distinguished Boston publishing house. After the firm bought the *Atlantic Monthly,* Fields followed James Russell Lowell as editor. Fields (twice a widower) ran a famous Boston literary salon with his third wife Annie, longtime friend and companion of writer Sarah Orne Jewett. The salon plays a major role in Van Wyck Brooks's *The Flowering of New England.*

Of his many poems, collected in several volumes, a ballad sometimes titled "The Tempest," and sometimes "The Captain's Daughter," contains the one memorable and oft-quoted line: " 'We are lost!' the Captain shouted, as he staggered down the stairs." As Merle Johnson points out in *You Know These Lines!* (1935), the captain, who is in the cabin, should have been on the bridge—and no one who served on a ship would call a ladder "the stairs."

Fields's most anthologized poem is the one that follows—a caustic blast at literary critics who are unable to recognize genuine art or poetry.

The Owl-Critic

"Who stuffed that white owl?" No one spoke in the shop:
The barber was busy, and he couldn't stop;
The customers, waiting their turns, were all reading
The *Daily,* the *Herald,* the *Post,* little heeding
The young man who blurted out such a blunt question;
Not one raised a head, or even made a suggestion;
　　　And the barber kept on shaving.

"Don't you see, Mister Brown,"
Cried the youth with a frown,
"How wrong the whole thing is,
How preposterous each wing is,
How flattened the head is, how jammed down the neck is—
In short, the whole owl, what an ignorant wreck 'tis!
I make no apology;
I've learned owl-eology.
I've passed days and nights in a hundred collections,
And cannot be blinded to any deflections
Arising from unskilful fingers that fail
To stuff a bird right, from his beak to his tail.
Mister Brown! Mister Brown!
Do take that bird down,
Or you'll soon be the laughing-stock all over town!"
　　　And the barber kept on shaving.

"I've *studied* owls
And other night fowls,
And I tell you
What I know to be true:
An owl cannot roost
With his limbs so unloosed;
No owl in this world
Ever had his claws curled,
Ever had his legs slanted,
Ever had his bill canted,
Ever had his neck screwed
Into that attitude.
He can't *do* it, because

'Tis against all bird-laws.
Anatomy teaches,
Ornithology preaches
An owl has a toe
That *can't* turn out so!
I've made the white owl my study for years,
And to see such a job almost moves me to tears!
Mister Brown, I'm amazed
You should be so gone crazed
As to put up a bird
In that posture absurd!
To *look* at that owl really brings on a dizziness;
The man who stuffed *him* don't half know his business!"
 And the barber kept on shaving.

"Examine those eyes.
I'm filled with surprise
Taxidermists should pass
Off on you such poor glass;
So unnatural they seem
They'd make Audubon scream,
And John Burroughs laugh
To encounter such chaff.
Do take that bird down;
Have him stuffed again, Brown!"
 And the barber kept on shaving.

"With some sawdust and bark
I could stuff in the dark
An owl better than that.
I could make an old hat
Look more like an owl
Than that horrid fowl,
Stuck up there so stiff like a side of coarse leather.
In fact, about *him* there's not one natural feather."
Just then, with a wink and a sly normal lurch,
The owl, very gravely, got down from his perch,
Walked round, and regarded his fault-finding critic
(Who thought he was stuffed) with a glance analytic
And then fairly hooted, as if he would say:
"Your learning's at fault *this* time, any way;
Don't waste it again on a live bird, I pray.
I'm an owl; you're another. Sir Critic, good-day!"
 And the barber kept on shaving.

FRANCIS MILES FINCH
(1827–1907)

BORN IN ITHACA, New York, and a Yale graduate, Finch became dean of the College of Law at Cornell University, after serving for a time as a judge on the New York Court of Appeals. His one claim to literary immortality, "The Blue and the Gray," first appeared in the *Atlantic Monthly* (September 1867). It is said to have been inspired by hearing about women who on Memorial Day put flowers on the graves of both Northern and Southern soldiers. Finch's book, *The Blue and the Gray and Other Verses* (1909), was posthumous. It seems incredible now that just a few generations ago the United States was engulfed in a civil war as bitter and bloody, perhaps as avoidable, as the latter-day conflict in what was Yugoslavia.

Julia Ward Howe's "Battle Hymn of the Republic" is, of course, the greatest of all poems inspired by the Civil War—it is in *Best Remembered Poems*—but Finch's impartial verse runs a close second. Finch's "The Blue and the Gray" was not the only poem with the same title. I have added here two others, both anonymous. I found the first in *The Speaker's Garland* 5, no. 20 (1881), and the second in Slason Thompson's anthology *The Humbler Poets* (1899).

The Blue and the Gray

By the flow of the inland river,
 Whence the fleets of iron have fled,
Where the blades of the grave-grass quiver,
 Asleep are the ranks of the dead:
 Under the sod and the dew,
 Waiting the judgment-day;
 Under the one, the Blue,
 Under the other, the Gray.

These in the robings of glory,
 Those in the gloom of defeat,
All with the battle-blood gory,
 In the dusk of eternity meet:
 Under the sod and the dew,
 Waiting the judgment-day;
 Under the laurel, the Blue,
 Under the willow, the Gray.

From the silence of sorrowful hours
 The desolate mourners go,
Lovingly laden with flowers

Alike for the friend and the foe:
 Under the sod and the dew,
 Waiting the judgment-day;
 Under the roses, the Blue,
 Under the lilies, the Gray.

So with an equal splendor,
 The morning sun-rays fall,
With a touch impartially tender,
 On the blossoms blooming for all:
 Under the sod and the dew,
 Waiting the judgment-day;
 Broidered with gold, the Blue,
 Mellowed with gold, the Gray.

So, when the summer calleth,
 On forest and field of grain,
With an equal murmur falleth
 The cooling drip of the rain:
 Under the sod and the dew,
 Waiting the judgment-day;
 Wet with the rain, the Blue,
 Wet with the rain, the Gray.

Sadly, but not with upbraiding,
 The generous deed was done,
In the storm of the years that are fading
 No braver battle was won:
 Under the sod and the dew,
 Waiting the judgment-day;
 Under the blossoms, the Blue,
 Under the garlands, the Gray.

No more shall the war cry sever,
 Or the winding rivers be red;
They banish our anger forever
 When they laurel the graves of our dead!
 Under the sod and the dew,
 Waiting the judgment-day;
 Love and tears for the Blue,
 Tears and love for the Gray.

The Blue and the Gray (Anonymous)

"O mother! what do they mean by blue?
 And what do they mean by gray?"
Was heard from the lips of a little child
 As she bounded in from play.
The mother's eyes filled up with tears;
 She turned to her darling fair,
And smoothed away from the sunny brow
 Its treasure of golden hair.

"Why, mother's eyes are blue, my sweet,
 And grandpa's hair is gray,
And the love we bear our darling child
 Grows stronger every day."
"But what did they mean?" persisted the child;
 "For I saw two cripples to-day,
And one of them said he fought for the blue,
 The other, he fought for the gray.

"Now, he of the blue had lost a leg,
 And the other had but one arm,
And both seemed worn and weary and sad,
 Yet their greeting was kind and warm.
They told of the battles in days gone by,
 Till it made my young blood thrill;
The leg was lost in the Wilderness fight,
 And the arm on Malvern Hill.

"They sat on the stone by the farm-yard gate,
 And talked for an hour or more,
Till their eyes grew bright and their hearts seemed warm
 With fighting their battles o'er;
And they parted at last with a friendly grasp,
 In a kindly, brotherly way,
Each calling on God to speed the time
 Uniting the blue and the gray."

Then the mother thought of other days,—
 Two stalwart boys from her riven;
How they knelt at her side and lispingly prayed,
 "Our Father which art in heaven;"
How one wore the gray and the other the blue;
 How they passed away from sight,

And had gone to the land where gray and blue
 Are merged in colors of light.

And she answered her darling with golden hair,
 While her heart was sadly wrung
With the thoughts awakened in that sad hour
 By her innocent prattling tongue:
"The blue and the gray are the colors of God,
 They are seen in the sky at even,
And many a noble, gallant soul
 Has found them a passport to heaven."

The Blue and the Gray (Anonymous)

Each thin hand resting on a grave,
 Her lips apart in prayer,
A mother knelt, and left her tears
 Upon the violets there.
O'er many a rood of vale and lawn,
 Of hill and forest gloom,
The reaper Death had revelled in
 His fearful harvest home.
The last unquiet summer shone
 Upon a fruitless fray;
From yonder forest charged the blue—
 Down yonder slope the gray.

The hush of death was on the scene,
 And sunset o'er the dead,
In that oppressive stillness,
 A pall of glory spread.
I know not, dare not question how
 I met the ghastly glare
Of each upturned and stirless face
 That shrunk and whitened there.
I knew my noble boys had stood
 Through all that withering day,
I knew that Willie wore the blue,
 That Harry wore the gray.

I thought of Willie's clear blue eye,
 His wavy hair of gold,

That clustered on a fearless brow
 Of purest Saxon mould;
Of Harry, with his raven locks
 And eagle glance of pride;
Of how they clasped each other's hand
 And left their mother's side;
How hand in hand they bore my prayers
 And blessings on the way—
A noble heart beneath the blue,
 Another 'neath the gray.

The dead, with white and folded hands,
 That hushed our village homes,
I 've seen laid calmly, tenderly,
 Within their darkened rooms;
But there I saw distorted limbs,
 And many an eye aglare,
In the soft purple twilight of
 The thunder-smitten air.
Along the slope and on the sward
 In ghastly ranks they lay,
And there was blood upon the blue
 And blood upon the gray.

I looked and saw his blood, and his;
 A swift and vivid dream
Of blended years flashed o'er me, when,
 Like some cold shadow, came
A blindness of the eye and brain—
 The same that seizes one
When men are smitten suddenly
 Who overstare the sun;
And while, blurred with the sudden stroke
 That swept my soul, I lay,
They buried Willie in his blue,
 And Harry in his gray.

The shadows fall upon their graves;
 They fall upon my heart;
And through the twilight of this soul
 Like dews the tears will start;
The starlight comes so silently
 And lingers where they rest;
So hope's revealing starlight sinks

And shines within my breast.
They ask not there, where yonder heaven
 Smiles with eternal day,
Why Willie wore the loyal blue,
 Why Harry wore the gray.

WILLIAM WESCOTT FINK
(1844–?)

I ATTACH FINK'S name to this narrative poem only because it is so credited in
The Speaker's Garland 7, no. 27 (1888). The poem is said to have appeared in
the New York *Independent,* but no date is given. In most later anthologies the
ballad is without a byline. All I could learn about Fink is that he published at
least two books of poems: *Valley Forge* (1870) and *Echoes from Erin* (1903).

Leadville, in central Colorado about 170 miles southwest of Denver, was one
of the most celebrated and turbulent mining camps in America. It experi-
enced both gold and silver booms. Horace Austin Warner Tabor (1820–1899),
known as "Silver Dollar Tabor," was the most famous of those prospectors who
made and lost huge fortunes mining silver in Leadville. After he died, his
second wife Elizabeth ("Baby Doe") Tabor, a notorious hooker, lived penni-
less near her husband's Matchless (but then worthless) Mine until she died of
exposure in 1935. Someone should write a ballad called "Leadville Liz."

Leadville Jim

He came to town one winter day;
He had walked from Leadville all the way;
He went to work in a lumber yard,
And wrote a letter that ran: "Dear Pard,
Stick to the claim, whatever you do,
And remember that Jim will see you through."
For, to quote his partner, "they owned a lead
Mid der shplendidest brospects, und nodings to ead."

When Sunday came he brushed his coat,
And tied a handkerchief round his throat,
Though his feet in hob-nailed shoes were shod,
He ventured to enter the house of God.

When, sharply scanning his ill-clad feet,
The usher gave him the rearmost seat.
By chance the loveliest girl in town

Came late to the house of God that day,
And, scorning to make a vain display
Of her brand new, beautiful Sunday gown,
Beside the threadbare man sat down.
When the organ pealed she turned to Jim,
And kindly offered her book to him,
Held half herself, and showed him the place,
And then, with genuine Christian grace,
She sang soprano, and he sang bass,
While up in the choir the basso growled,
The tenor, soprano, and alto howled,
And the banker's son looked back and scowled.

The preacher closed his sermon grand
With an invitation to "join the band."
Then quietly from his seat uprose
The miner, dressed in his threadbare clothes,
And over the carpeted floor walked down,
The aisle of the richest church in town.
In spite of the general shudder and frown,
He joined the church and went his way;
But he did not know he had walked that day
O'er the sensitive corns of pride, rough-shod;
For the miner was thinking just then of God.
A little lonely it seemed to him
In the rearmost pew when Sunday came;
One deacon had dubbed him "Leadville Jim,"
But the rest had forgotten quite his name.

And yet 'twas never more strange than true,
God sat with the man in the rearmost pew,
Strengthened his arm in the lumber yard,
And away in the mountains helped his "Pard."

But after awhile a letter came
Which ran: "Dear Yim—I haf sell our claim,
Und I send you a jeck for half der same.
A million, I dought, was a pooty good brice,
Und my *heart* said to sell, so I took its advice—
You know what I mean if you lofe a fraulein—
Good-bye. I am going to marry Katrine."

The hob-nailed shoes and rusty coat
Were laid aside, and another note
Came rippling out of the public throat,
The miner was now no longer "Jim,"

But the deacons "Brothered" and "Mistered" him;
Took their buggies and showed him round.
And, more than the fact of his wealth, they found
Through the papers which told the wondrous tale,
That the fellow had led his class at Yale.
Ah! the maidens admired his splendid shape,
Which the tailor had matched with careful tape;
But he married the loveliest girl in town,
The one who once by his side sat down,
When up in the choir the basso growled,
Then tenor, soprano, and alto howled,
And the banker's son looked back and scowled.

HARRIET A. GLAZEBROOK
(?–?)

ALL I KNOW about Glazebrook is that she was a British temperance leader who wrote anti-booze verse and edited collections with such titles as *Readings and Recitations, Chiefly upon Temperance* (London, 1874) and *Readings in Rhyme from the Drama of Drink* (London, 1876).

Glazebrook did not invent the ringing declaration "Lips that touch liquor shall never touch mine." This was adapted from an earlier poem by one George W. Young, about whom I also know nothing. His poem seems to have been first published as a broadside about 1870. The version given here is from *The Speaker's Garland* 4, no. 16 (1878). Both poems were popular recitations at temperance meetings in the United States and in England.

Today it is easy to ridicule the temperance movement, when leaders smashed saloon windows with axes, and to forget that it arose when liquor was the scourge of the land. More people died then from alcoholism than they do today from smoking. There is a strong parallel between the two addictions. Restaurants in pre-prohibition days took pride in being alcohol-free just as an increasing number now take pride in being smoke-free. Both men and women today are saying, "Lips that touch tobacco shall never touch mine."

Lips That Touch Liquor Shall Never Touch Mine

Alice Lee stood awaiting her lover one night,
Her cheeks flushed and glowing, her eyes full of light.
She had placed a sweet rose 'mid her wild flowing hair;

No flower of the forest e'er looked half so fair
As she did that night, as she stood by the door
Of the cot where she dwelt by the side of the moor.

She heard a quick step coming over the moor,
And a merry voice which she had oft heard before;
And ere she could speak a strong arm held her fast,
And a manly voice whispered, "I've come, love, at last.
I'm sorry that I've kept you waiting like this,
But I know you'll forgive me, then give me a kiss."

But she shook the bright curls on her beautiful head,
And she drew herself up while quite proudly she said,
"Now, William, I'll prove if you really are true,
For you say that you love me—I don't think you do;
If really you love me you must give up the wine,
For the lips that touch liquor shall never touch mine."

He looked quite amazed. "Why, Alice, 'tis clear
You really are getting quite jealous, my dear."
"In that you are right," she replied; "for, you see,
You'll soon love the liquor far better than me.
I'm jealous, I own, of the poisonous wine,
For the lips that touch liquor shall never touch mine."

He turned, then, quite angry. "Confound it!" he said,
"What nonsense you've got in your dear little head;
But I'll see if I cannot remove it from hence."
She said, "'Tis not nonsense, 'tis plain common-sense:
And I mean what I say, and this you will find,
I don't often change when I've made up my mind."

He stood all irresolute, angry, perplexed:
She never before saw him look half so vexed;
But she said, "If he talks all his life I won't flinch";
And he talked, but he never could move her an inch.
He then bitterly cried, with a look and a groan,
"O Alice, your heart is as hard as a stone."

But though her heart beat in his favour quite loud,
She still firmly kept to the vow she had vowed;
And at last, without even a tear or a sigh,
She said, "I am going, so, William, goodbye."
"Nay, stay," he then said, "I'll choose one of the two—
I'll give up the liquor in favour of you."

Now, William had often great cause to rejoice
For the hour he had made sweet Alice his choice;
And he blessed through the whole of a long, useful life,
The fate that had given him his dear little wife.
And she, by her firmness, won to us that night
One who in our cause is an ornament bright.

Oh! that each fair girl in our abstinence band
Would say: "I'll ne'er give my heart or my hand
Unto one who I ever had reason to think
Would taste one small drop of the vile, cursed drink";
But say, when you are wooed, "I'm a foe to the wine,
And the lips that touch liquor shall never touch mine."

Lips That Touch Liquor Must Never Touch Mine (by George W. Young)

You are coming to woo me, but not as of yore,
When I hastened to welcome your ring at the door;
For I trusted that he who stood waiting me then,
Was the brightest, the truest, the noblest of men.
Your lips, on my own when they printed "Farewell,"
Had never been soiled by "the beverage of hell;"
But they come to me now with the bacchanal sign,
And the lips that touch liquor must never touch mine.

I think of that night in the garden alone,
When in whispers you told me your heart was my own,
That your love in the future should faithfully be
Unshared by another, kept only for me.
Oh, sweet to my soul is the memory still,
Of the lips which met mine, when they murmured "I will;"
But now to their pressure no more they incline,
For the lips that touch liquor must never touch mine!

O John! how it crushed me, when first in your face
The pen of the "Rum Fiend" had written "disgrace;"
And turned me in silence and tears from that breath
All poisoned and foul from the chalice of death.
It scattered the hopes I had treasured to last;
It darkened the future and clouded the past;
It shattered my idol, and ruined the shrine,
For the lips that touch liquor must never touch mine.

I loved you—Oh, dearer than language can tell,
And you saw it, you proved it, you knew it too well!
But the man of my love was far other than he
Who now from the "Tap-room" comes reeling to me:
In manhood and honor so noble and right—
His heart was so true, and his genius so bright—
And his soul was unstained, unpolluted by wine;
But the lips that touch liquor must never touch mine.

You promised reform, but I trusted in vain;
Your pledge was but made to be broken again:
And the lover so false to his promises now,
Will not, as a husband, be true to his vow.
The word must be spoken that bids you depart—
Though the effort to speak it should shatter my heart—
Though in silence, with blighted affection, I pine,
Yet the lips that touch liquor must never touch mine!

If one spark, in your bosom, of virtue remain,
Go fan it with prayer till it kindle again;
Resolved, with "God helping," in future to be
From wine and its follies unshackled and free!
And when you have conquered this foe of your soul,—
In manhood and honor beyond his control—
This heart will again beat responsive to thine,
And the lips free from liquor be welcome to mine.

HOMER GREENE
(1853–1940)

HOMER GREENE IS another splendid specimen of what Burton Stevenson, in *Famous Single Poems*, calls a "one-poem poet." According to an entry in *Who Was Who*, he was a Honesdale, Pennsylvania lawyer—director of a local bank and a cemetery, and active in state politics. He wrote at least fifteen books of prose, and one book of verse, *What My Lover Said* (1931).

The title poem is the only one worth remembering. It first appeared in the New York *Evening Post* (November 19, 1875). An editor changed the title from "What Her Lover Said," and gave it the byline of H. G. As the poem got reprinted here and there, and recited by professional "speakers," some editor decided that H. G. stood for Horace Greeley, who died in 1872! In vain Greene tried to quash the mistake. On December 8, 1880, the *Evening Post* published a long letter in which Greene said he wrote the poem when he was a student at Union College.

In 1886, another name was put forward as that of the poem's author, Colonel Richard Realf. Realf had killed himself in 1879, but his friends insisted in letters to the Philadelphia *News* that he was the poem's true author.

The most annoying claimant was Mrs. O. C. Jones, a wealthy woman in Abbeville, Louisiana, who informed the New York *Sun* that she had penned the poem about a Confederate soldier with whom she had a torrid romance. Greene offered his home in Honesdale to anyone who could prove the poem was published before 1875, but Mrs. Jones refused to give in. In more letters to the *Sun* she insisted it was a Union soldier with whom she had flirted, and to whom she gave a copy of her poem. She could not remember his name, but surely it was he who passed the gem on to the *Evening Post*.

Mrs. Jones then made a fatal mistake. To prove she wrote the poem she offered a sequel, titled "A Twilight Dream." It was so awful that the *Sun* finally stopped defending her. As Stevenson puts it, "she slipped into . . . peaceful obscurity."

What My Lover Said

By the merest chance, in the twilight gloom,
 In the orchard path he met me;
In the tall, wet grass, with its faint perfume,
And I tried to pass, but he made no room,
 Oh, I tried, but he would not let me.
So I stood and blushed till the grass grew red,
 With my face bent down above it,
While he took my hand as he whispering said—
(How the clover lifted each pink, sweet head,
To listen to all that my lover said;
 Oh, the clover in bloom, I love it!)

In the high, wet grass went the path to hide,
 And the low, wet leaves hung over;
But I could not pass upon either side,
For I found myself, when I vainly tried,
 In the arms of my steadfast lover.
And he held me there and he raised my head,
 While he closed the path before me,
And he looked down into my eyes and said—
(How the leaves bent down from the boughs o'er head,
To listen to all that my lover said;
 Oh, the leaves hanging lowly o'er me!)

Had he moved aside but a little way,
 I could surely then have passed him;

And he knew I never could wish to stay,
And would not have heard what he had to say,
 Could I only aside have cast him.
It was almost dark, and the moments sped,
 And the searching night wind found us,
But he drew me nearer and softly said—
(How the pure, sweet wind grew still, instead,
To listen to all that my lover said;
 Oh, the whispering wind around us!)

I am sure that he knew when he held me fast,
 That I must be all unwilling;
For I tried to go, and I would have passed,
As the night was come with its dew, at last,
 And the sky with its stars was filling.
But he clasped me close when I would have fled,
 And he made me hear his story,
And his soul came out from his lips and said—
(How the stars crept out where the white moon led,
To listen to all that my lover said;
 Oh, the moon and the stars in glory!)

I know that the grass and the leaves will not tell,
 And I'm sure that the wind, precious rover,
Will carry my secret so safely and well
 That no being shall ever discover
One word of the many that rapidly fell
 From the soul-speaking lips of my lover;
 And the moon and the stars that looked over
Shall never reveal what a fairy-like spell
They wove round about us that night in the dell,
 In the path through the dew-laden clover,
Nor echo the whispers that made my heart swell
 As they fell from the lips of my lover.

BRET HARTE
(1839–1902)

FRANCIS BRET HARTE was born in Albany, New York. After a series of jobs in California, including gold mining and printing, he settled in San Francisco to become a popular writer of novels, short stories, poems and amusing parodies. One of his parodies was a mystery story involving Hemlock Jones. Of his two

failed plays, *Ah Sin* was written with Mark Twain. In later years he lived in several eastern cities, and finally in London. He wrote more than forty books, and his *Collected Writings* (1904) fill nineteen volumes.

Harte's poem about the Chinese card hustler, usually titled "The Heathen Chinee," first appeared in the *Overland Monthly* (September 1870), while Harte was editor. It was reprinted the following year by Western News, of Chicago, on a set of nine cards illustrated by Joseph Hall. It was also published that year as a pamphlet, with pictures by Sol Eytinge, Jr., and included in a cloth-bound volume, *Poems by Bret Harte*. The poem was set to music by at least two composers, Charles Towner and F. Boott. It is surely the most famous poem ever written about euchre. In this card game a "bower" is one of the two highest cards unless a joker is used, in which case it is the second or third highest. The "bowers" are the jack of trumps, called the "right bower," and the jack of the same color, called the "left bower." The wax on Ah Sin's fingernails was secretly used for marking cards. Harte wrote the poem during America's obsession with the "Yellow Peril," a fear of China intensified by the flood of Chinese laborers who worked for low pay on the railroads that opened up the west. The phrase "the heathen Chinee is peculiar" was bandied about the country for many years.

I found an anonymous reply to Truthful James, spoken by Ah Sin, in *The Speaker's Garland* 1, no. 4 (1872), Choice Selections, and have included it here.

"Her Letter" and "His Answer" first appeared in the *Overland Monthly* in 1870. "Her Last Letter," rounding out the romance, was written much later. In 1905 Houghton Mifflin posthumously published the trilogy in a book handsomely illustrated with more than 45 plates, some in full color, by Arthur I. Keller.

Plain Language from Truthful James

Which I wish to remark,
 And my language is plain,
That for ways that are dark
 And for tricks that are vain,
The heathen Chinee is peculiar,
 Which the same I would rise to explain.

Ah Sin was his name;
 And I shall not deny,
In regard to the same,
 What that name might imply;
But his smile it was pensive and childlike,
 As I frequent remarked to Bill Nye.

It was August the third,
 And quite soft was the skies;

Which it might be inferred
 That Ah Sin was likewise;
Yet he played it that day upon William
 And me in a way I despise.

Which we had a small game,
 And Ah Sin took a hand:
It was Euchre. The same
 He did not understand;
But he smiled as he sat by the table,
 With the smile that was childlike and bland.

Yet the cards they were stocked
 In a way that I grieve,
And my feelings were shocked
 At the state of Nye's sleeve,
Which was stuffed full of aces and bowers,
 And the same with intent to deceive.

But the hands that were played
 By that heathen Chinee,
And the points that he made,
 Were quite frightful to see,—
Till at last he put down a right bower,
 Which the same Nye had dealt unto me.

Then I looked up at Nye,
 And he gazed upon me;
And he rose with a sigh,
 And said, "Can this be?
We are ruined by Chinese cheap labor,"—
 And he went for that heathen Chinee.

In the scene that ensued
 I did not take a hand,
But the floor it was strewed
 Like the leaves on the strand
With the cards that Ah Sin had been hiding,
 In the game "he did not understand."

In his sleeves, which were long,
 He had twenty-four jacks,—
Which was coming it strong,
 Yet I state but the facts;
And we found on his nails, which were taper,
 What is frequent in tapers,—that's wax.

Which is why I remark,
 And my language is plain,
That for ways that are dark
 And for tricks that are vain,
The heathen Chinee is peculiar,—
 Which the same I am free to maintain.

Ah Sin's Reply (Anonymous)

Which my name is Ah Sin;
 I don't want to call names,
But I must, to begin,
 Say of this T. James:
That I am convinced he is rather
 Well up in the sinfullest games.

Yes, Ah Sin is my name,
 Which I need not deny;
What it means is no shame,
 You will find, if you try,
That its meaning is something Celestial,
 And how is Celestial for High?

And about that small game
 I did not understand,
So I made it my aim,
 With a smile that was bland,
To keep my small eyes at their keenest
 On Nye as he dealt the first hand.

And the way that he dealt,
 There could nothing be finer;
But somehow I felt,
 "Mr. Ah Sin, from China,
Because your smile is so childlike,
 These fellows play you for a minor!"

But no slouch is Ah Sin,
 And from the word "Go!"
I did play for to win,
 And Nye—rather so;
And I played the new game as I learned him,
 Which showed level head, don't you know?

On my nails there was wax,
 But that nothing proves,
When I state the real facts;
 I was 'prenticed on shoes,
And the wax that was found on my fingers
 Was the kind that our shoemakers use.

And the packs up my sleeve,
 My oath I will take,
Were not there to deceive,
 But got there by mistake;
I bought them for Ah Sin, the younger,
 Who likes some card houses to make.

In my pockets they were
 When I sat down that day;
But what with the stir
 And excitement of play,
They worked up my sleeve from my pocket,
 And strange it was, too, I must say.

Was it right in Bill Nye
 When the trump knave I led,
To blacken my eye,
 And on me put a head?
Had I known James held the right bower
 I'd have played something else in its stead.

But I don't play no more,
 For my lot now is cast
On a euchreless shore,
 So I "stick" to my "last,"
And my smile, at North Adams, is pensive
 At my heathenish days that are past.

Her Letter

I'm sitting alone by the fire,
 Dressed just as I came from the dance,
In a robe even *you* would admire,—
 It cost a cool thousand in France;
I'm be-diamonded out of all reason,
 My hair is done up in a cue:

In short, sir, "the belle of the season"
 Is wasting an hour upon you.

A dozen engagements I've broken;
 I left in the midst of a set;
Likewise a proposal, half spoken,
 That waits—on the stairs—for me yet.
They say he'll be rich,—when he grows up,—
 And then he adores me indeed;
And you, sir, are turning your nose up,
 Three thousand miles off, as you read.

"And how do I like my position?"
 "And what do I think of New York?"
"And now, in my higher ambition,
 With whom do I waltz, flirt, or talk?"
"And is n't it nice to have riches,
 And diamonds and silks, and all that?"
"And are n't they a change to the ditches
 And tunnels of Poverty Flat?"

Well, yes,—if you saw us out driving
 Each day in the Park, four-in-hand,
If you saw poor dear mamma contriving
 To look supernaturally grand,—
If you saw papa's picture, as taken
 By Brady, and tinted at that,—
You'd never suspect he sold bacon
 And flour at Poverty Flat.

And yet, just this moment, when sitting
 In the glare of the grand chandelier,—
In the bustle and glitter befitting
 The "finest *soirée* of the year,"—
In the mists of a *gaze de Chambéry*,
 And the hum of the smallest of talk,—
Somehow, Joe, I thought of the "Ferry,"
 And the dance that we had on "The Fork;"

Of Harrison's barn, with its muster
 Of flags festooned over the wall;
Of the candles that shed their soft lustre
 And tallow on head-dress and shawl;
Of the steps that we took to one fiddle,
 Of the dress of my queer *vis-à-vis;*

And how I once went down the middle
 With the man that shot Sandy McGee;

Of the moon that was quietly sleeping
 On the hill, when the time came to go;
Of the few baby peaks that were peeping
 From under their bedclothes of snow;
Of that ride,—that to me was the rarest;
 Of—the something you said at the gate.
Ah! Joe, then I was n't an heiress
 To "the best-paying lead in the State."

Well, well, it's all past; yet it's funny
 To think, as I stood in the glare
Of fashion and beauty and money,
 That I should be thinking, right there,
Of some one who breasted high water,
 And swam the North Fork, and all that,
Just to dance with old Folinsbee's daughter,
 The Lily of Poverty Flat.

But goodness! what nonsense I'm writing!
 (Mamma says my taste still is low),
Instead of my triumphs reciting,
 I'm spooning on Joseph,—heigh-ho!
And I'm to be "finished" by travel,—
 Whatever's the meaning of that.
Oh, why did papa strike pay gravel
 In drifting on Poverty Flat?

Good-night!—here's the end of my paper;
 Good-night!—if the longitude please,—
For maybe, while wasting my taper,
 Your sun's climbing over the trees.[1]
But know, if you have n't got riches,
 And are poor, dearest Joe, and all that,
That my heart's somewhere there in the ditches,
 And you 've struck it,—on Poverty Flat.

[1] *Your . . . trees*] The lady blundered here. If she is writing at night, in New York, after a dance, it would be three hours *earlier* in California, hardly a time of sunrise. She wrongly assumed that time in California is three hours ahead of New York time, rather than three hours behind.

His Answer (Reported by Truthful James)

Being asked by an intimate party,—
 Which the same I would term as a friend,—
Though his health it were vain to call hearty,
 Since the mind to deceit it might lend;
For his arm it was broken quite recent,
 And there's something gone wrong with his lung,—
Which is why it is proper and decent
 I should write what he runs off his tongue.

First, he says, Miss, he's read through your letter
 To the end,—and "the end came too soon;"
That a "slight illness kept him your debtor,"
 (Which for weeks he was wild as a loon);
That "his spirits are buoyant as yours is;"
 That with you, Miss, he "challenges Fate,"
(Which the language that invalid uses
 At times it were vain to relate).

And he says "that the mountains are fairer
 For once being held in your thought;"
That each rock "holds a wealth that is rarer
 Than ever by gold-seeker sought."
(Which are words he would put in these pages,
 By a party not given to guile;
Though the claim not, at date, paying wages,
 Might produce in the sinful a smile.)

He remembers the ball at the Ferry,
 And the ride, and the gate, and the vow,
And the rose that you gave him,—that very
 Same rose he is "treasuring now."
(Which his blanket he's kicked on his trunk, Miss,
 And insists on his legs being free;
And his language to me from his bunk, Miss,
 Is frequent and painful and free.)

He hopes you are wearing no willows,
 But are happy and gay all the while;
That he knows—(which this dodging of pillows
 Imparts but small ease to the style,
And the same you will pardon)—he knows, Miss,
 That, though parted by many a mile,
"Yet, were *he* lying under the snows, Miss,
 They'd melt into tears at your smile."

And "you'll still think of him in your pleasures,
 In your brief twilight dreams of the past;
In this green laurel spray that he treasures,—
 It was plucked where your parting was last;
In this specimen,—but a small trifle,—
 It will do for a pin for your shawl."
(Which, the truth not to wickedly stifle,
 Was his last week's "clean up,"—and *his all*.)

He's asleep, which the same might seem strange, Miss,
 Were it not that I scorn to deny
That I raised his last dose, for a change, Miss,
 In view that his fever was high;
But he lies there quite peaceful and pensive.
 And now, my respects, Miss, to you;
Which my language, although comprehensive,
 Might seem to be freedom, is true.

For I have a small favor to ask you,
 As concerns a bull-pup, and the same,—
If the duty would not overtask you,—
 You would please to procure for me, *game;*
And send per express to the Flat, Miss,—
 For they say York is famed for the breed,
Which, though words of deceit may be that, Miss,
 I'll trust to your taste, Miss, indeed.

P.S.—Which this same interfering
 Into other folks' way I despise;
Yet if it so be I was hearing
 That it's just empty pockets as lies
Betwixt you and Joseph, it follers
 That, having no family claims,
Here's my pile, which it's six hundred dollars,
 As is *yours*, with respects,
 Truthful James.

Her Last Letter

June 4th! Do you know what that date means?
 June 4th! By this air and these pines!
Well,—only you know how I hate scenes,—
 These might be my very last lines!

For perhaps, sir, you'll kindly remember—
 If some *other* things you've forgot—
That you last wrote the 4th of *December*,—
 Just six months ago!—from this spot;

From this spot, that you said was "the fairest
 For once being held in my thought."
Now, really I call that the barest
 Of—well, I won't say what I ought!
For here *I* am back from my "riches,"
 My "triumphs," my "tours," and all that;
And *you're* not to be found in the ditches
 Or temples of Poverty Flat!

From Paris we went for the season
 To London, when pa wired, "Stop."
Mama says "his *health*" was the reason.
 (I've heard that some things took a "drop.")
But she said if my patience I'd summon
 I could go back with him to the Flat—
Perhaps I was thinking of some one
 Who of me—well—was not thinking *that*!

Of course you will *say* that I "never
 Replied to the letter you wrote."
That is just like a man! But, however,
 I read it—or how could I quote?
And as to the stories you've heard (No,
 Don't tell me you have n't—I know!),
You'll not believe one blessed word, Joe;
 But just whence they came, let them go!

And they came from Sade Lotski of Yolo,
 Whose father sold clothes on the Bar—
You called him Job-lotski, you know, Joe,
 And the boys said *her* value was *par.*
Well, we met her in Paris—just flaring
 With diamonds, and lost in a hat!
And she asked me "How Joseph was faring
 In his love-suit on Poverty Flat!"

She thought it would shame me! I met her
 With a look, Joe, that made her eyes drop;
And I said that your "love-suit fared better
 Than any suit out of *their* shop!"

And I did n't blush *then*—as I'm doing
 To find myself here, all alone,
And left, Joe, to do all the "sueing"
 To a lover that's certainly flown.

In this brand-new hotel, called "The Lily"
 (I wonder who gave it that name?),
I really am feeling quite silly,
 To think I was once called the same;
And I stare from its windows, and fancy
 I'm labeled to each passer-by.
Ah! gone is the old necromancy,
 For nothing seems right to my eye.

On that hill there are stores that I knew not;
 There's a street—where I once lost my way;
And the copse where you once tied my shoe-knot
 Is shamelessly open as day!
And that bank by the spring—I once drank there,
 And you called the place Eden, you know;
Now I'm banished like Eve—though the bank there
 Is belonging to "Adams and Co."

There's the rustle of silk on the sidewalk;
 Just now there passed by a tall hat;
But there's gloom in this "boom" and this wild talk
 Of the "future" of Poverty Flat.
There's a decorous chill in the air, Joe,
 Where once we were simple and free;
And I hear they've been making a mayor, Joe,
 Of the man who shot Sandy McGee.

But there's still the "lap, lap" of the river;
 There's the song of the pines, deep and low.
(How my longing for them made me quiver
 In the park that they call Fontainebleau!)
There's the snow-peak that looked on our dances,
 And blushed when the morning said, "Go!"
There's a lot that remains which one fancies—
 But somehow there's never a Joe!

Perhaps, on the whole, it is better,
 For you might have been changed like the rest;
Though it's strange that I'm trusting this letter
 To papa, just to have it addressed.

He thinks he may find you, and really
 Seems kinder now I'm all alone.
You might have been here, Joe, if merely
 To *look* what I'm willing to *own.*

Well, well! that's all past; so good-night, Joe;
 Good-night to the river and Flat;
Good-night to what's wrong and what's right, Joe;
 Good-night to the past, and all that—
To Harrison's barn, and its dancers;
 To the moon, and the white peak of snow;
And good-night to the cañon that answers
 My "Joe!" with its echo of "No!"

<center>P. S.</center>

I've just got your note. You deceiver!
 How dared you—how *could* you? Oh, Joe!
To think I've been kept a believer
 In things that were six months ago!
And it's *you*'ve built this house, and the bank, too,
 And the mills, and the stores, and all that!
And for everything changed I must thank *you,*
 Who have "struck it" on Poverty Flat!

How dared you get rich—you great stupid!—
 Like papa, and some men that I know,
Instead of just trusting to Cupid
 And to me for your money? Ah, Joe!
Just to think you sent never a word, dear,
 Till you wrote to papa for consent!
Now I know why they had me transferred here,
 And "the health of papa"—what *that* meant!

Now I know why they call this "The Lily;"
 Why the man who shot Sandy McGee
You made mayor! 'T was because—oh, you silly!—
 He once "went down the middle" with me!
I've been fooled to the top of my bent here,
 So come, and ask pardon—you know
That you've still got to get *my* consent, dear!
 And just think what that echo said—Joe!

JOHN (MILTON) HAY
(1838–1905)

BORN IN SALEM, Indiana, attorney John Hay began his distinguished political career as Lincoln's assistant private secretary. A ten-volume biography of Lincoln (1890), which he wrote with John Nicolay, is a basic reference on Lincoln's life. Hay's last government post was Secretary of State from 1898 until his death.

No one today reads Hay's novel *The Bread-winners,* or the western dialect doggerel in his *Pike County Ballads and Other Pieces* (1871). The one poem in that book that became enormously popular was "Jim Bludso," with "Little Breeches" running second. His *Complete Poetical Works* was published posthumously.

"Jim Bludso" was first printed in the New York *Semi-Weekly Tribune* (January 6, 1871), a newspaper on which Hay worked at the time. Its second appearance was in a pamphlet titled *Jim Bludso of the Prairie Belle, and Little Breeches* (1871), with illustrations by Sol Eytinge, Jr.

Robert Service paid tribute to "Jim Bludso" in the third stanza of "The Test":

> Some poems lift aloft the mind,
> Some whisper to the heart;
> Unto the last I'm more inclined,
> Though innocent of art.
> Some verses get beneath my skin—
> Like *Casey at the Bat,*
> Or *Jim Bludso* or *Gunga Din*—
> Why didn't I write that?

Bludso also turns up in James Joyce's *Ulysses* (Vintage edition, 1961, page 458): "I did all a white man could. (*With quiet feeling.*) Jim Bludso. Hold her nozzle again the bank."

The poem is said to have been based on the sinking of the Mississippi River steamboat *Fashion,* and the death of its engineer Oliver Fairchild. "Pike," in the second stanza, is Pike County, Missouri.

Joe Mitchell Chapple, editor of *Favorite Heart Throbs of Famous People,* wrote that Ella Wheeler Wilcox, "in answer to my query as to her favorite poem, copied out and sent in the poem of John Hay, 'The Stirrup-Cup.' " It, too, appears in many anthologies.

"Stirrup-cup" was a term for a farewell drink, usually wine, offered to a rider just before he mounted his horse. In Hay's lyric the horse is, of course, death.

Jim Bludso of the Prairie Belle

Wall, no! I can't tell whar he lives,
 Becase he don't live, you see;
Leastways, he's got out of the habit

Of livin' like you and me.
Whar have you been for the last three year
 That you haven't heard folks tell
How Jimmy Bludso passed in his checks
 The night of the Prairie Belle?

He weren't no saint,—them engineers
 Is all pretty much alike,—
One wife in Natchez-under-the-Hill
 And another one here, in Pike;
A keerless man in his talk was Jim,
 And an awkward hand in a row,
But he never flunked, and he never lied,—
 I reckon he never knowed how.

And this was all the religion he had,—
 To treat his engine well;
Never be passed on the river;
 To mind the pilot's bell;
And if ever the Prairie Belle took fire,—
 A thousand times he swore
He'd hold her nozzle agin the bank
 Till the last soul got ashore.

All boats has their day on the Mississip,
 And her day come at last,—
The Movastar was a better boat,
 But the Belle she *wouldn't* be passed.
And so she come tearin' along that night—
 The oldest craft on the line—
With a nigger squat on her safety-valve,
 And her furnace crammed, rosin and pine.

The fire burst out as she clared the bar,
 And burnt a hole in the night,
And quick as a flash she turned, and made
 For that willer-bank on the right.
There was runnin' and cursin', but Jim yelled out,
 Over all the infernal roar,
"I'll hold her nozzle agin the bank
 Till the last galoot's ashore."

Through the hot, black breath of the burnin' boat
 Jim Bludso's voice was heard,
And they all had trust in his cussedness,
 And knowed he would keep his word.

And, sure's you're born, they all got off
 Afore the smokestacks fell,—
And Bludso's ghost went up alone
 In the smoke of the Prairie Belle.

He weren't no saint,—but at jedgment
 I'd run my chance with Jim,
'Longside of some pious gentleman
 That wouldn't shake hands with him.
He seen his duty, a dead-sure thing,—
 And went for it thar and then;
And Christ ain't a going to be too hard
 On a man that died for men.

The Stirrup-Cup

My short and happy day is done,
The long and dreary night comes on,
And at my door the pale horse stands
To carry me to unknown lands.

His whinny shrill, his pawing hoof,
Sound dreadful as a gathering storm;
And I must leave this sheltering roof
And joys of life so soft and warm.

Tender and warm the joys of life,—
Good friends, the faithful and the true;
My rosy children and my wife,
So sweet to kiss, so fair to view,—

So sweet to kiss, so fair to view:
The night comes down, the lights burn blue;
And at my door the pale horse stands
To bear me forth to unknown lands.

J. MILTON HAYES
(?–?)

ACCORDING TO Michael Turner, in *Parlour Poetry* (1967 edition), this tragic tale of Mad Carew was first published in 1911 in *Reynold's Musical Monologues,* with music by Cuthbert Clarke, and was a favorite recitation of Bransby Williams, a music-hall entertainer.

Alec Waugh, in *My Brother Evelyn and Other Profiles,* identifies Hayes as a North Country actor, and quotes him as saying:

"I wrote 'The Green Eye of the Little Yellow God' in five hours, but I had it all planned out. It isn't poetry and it does not pretend to be, but it does what it sets out to do. It appeals to the imagination from the start: those colours, green and yellow, create an atmosphere. Then India, everyone has his own idea of India. Don't tell the public too much. Strike chords. It's no good describing a house; the reader will fix the scene in some spot he knows himself. All you've got to say is 'India' and a man sees something. Then play on his susceptibilities.

" 'His name was Mad Carew.' You've got the whole man there. The public will fill in the picture for you. And then the mystery. Leave enough unsaid to make paterfamilias pat himself on the back, 'I've spotted it, he can't fool me. I'm up to that dodge. I know where he went.' No need to explain. Then that final ending where you began. It carries people back. You've got a compact whole."

I was unable to learn anything further about Hayes, not even his birth and death years, and would be grateful to anyone who can tell me something about him. Is this the only poem he wrote?

The Green Eye of the Little Yellow God

There's a one-eyed yellow idol to the north of Khatmandu,
There's a little marble cross below the town;
There's a broken-hearted woman tends the grave of Mad Carew,
And the Yellow God forever gazes down.

He was known as "Mad Carew" by the subs at Khatmandu,
He was hotter than they felt inclined to tell;
But for all his foolish pranks, he was worshipped in the ranks,
And the Colonel's daughter smiled on him as well.

He had loved her all along, with a passion of the strong,
The fact that she loved him was plain to all.
She was nearly twenty-one and arrangements had begun
To celebrate her birthday with a ball.

He wrote to ask what present she would like from Mad Carew;
They met next day as he dismissed a squad;
And jestingly she told him then that nothing else would do
But the green eye of the little Yellow God.

On the night before the dance, Mad Carew seemed in a
 trance,
And they chaffed him as they puffed at their cigars;
But for once he failed to smile, and he sat alone awhile,
Then went out into the night beneath the stars.

He returned before the dawn, with his shirt and tunic torn,
And a gash across his temple dripping red;
He was patched up right away, and he slept through all the
 day,
And the Colonel's daughter watched beside his bed.

He woke at last and asked if they could send his tunic
 through;
She brought it, and he thanked her with a nod;
He bade her search the pocket saying, "That's from Mad
 Carew,"
And she found the little green eye of the god.

She upbraided poor Carew in the way that women do,
Though both her eyes were strangely hot and wet;
But she wouldn't take the stone and Mad Carew was left alone
With the jewel that he'd chanced his life to get.

When the ball was at its height, on that still and tropic night,
She thought of him and hastened to his room;
As she crossed the barrack square she could hear the dreamy
 air
Of a waltz tune softly stealing thro' the gloom.

His door was open wide, with silver moonlight shining
 through;
The place was wet and slipp'ry where she trod;
An ugly knife lay buried in the heart of Mad Carew,
'Twas the "Vengeance of the Little Yellow God."

There's a one-eyed yellow idol to the north of Khatmandu,
There's a little marble cross below the town;
There's a broken-hearted woman tends the grave of Mad
 Carew,
And the Yellow God forever gazes down.

GEORGE HOEY
(?–?)

I HAVE LEARNED nothing about George Hoey, or if he is indeed the author of "Asleep at the Switch," or whether the name is a pseudonym. He is credited for the ballad in *The Speaker's Garland* 4, no. 16 (1879), and in many later "speakers," though usually the poem is without a byline. There are slight differences of words and punctuation in various reprintings of the poem. The version here is from the anthology cited.

Asleep at the Switch

The first thing that I remember was Carlo tugging away
With the sleeve of my coat fast in his teeth, pulling, as much as
 to say:
"Come, master, awake, attend to the switch, lives now depend
 upon you,
Think of the souls in the coming train, and the graves you are
 sending them to.
Think of the mother and the babe at her breast, think of the
 father and son,
Think of the lover and loved one too, think of them doomed
 every one
To fall (as it were by your very hand) into yon fathomless
 ditch,
Murdered by one who should guard them from harm, who
 now lies asleep at the switch."

I sprang up amazed—scarce knew where I stood, sleep had
 o'ermastered me so;
I could hear the wind hollowly howling, and the deep river
 dashing below,
I could hear the forest leaves rustling, as the trees by the
 tempest were fanned,
But what was that noise in the distance? That, I could not
 understand.
I heard it at first indistinctly, like the rolling of some muffled
 drum,
Then nearer and nearer it came to me, till it made my very
 ears hum;

What is this light that surrounds me and seems to set fire to
my brain?
What whistle's that, yelling so shrill? Ah! I know now; it's the
train.

We often stand facing some danger and seem to take root to
the place;
So I stood—with this demon before me, its heated breath
scorching my face;
Its headlight made day of the darkness and glared like the eyes
of some witch,—
The train was almost upon me before I remembered the
switch.
I sprang to it, seizing it wildly, the train dashing fast down the
track;
The switch resisted my efforts, some devil seemed holding it
back;
On, on came the fiery-eyed monster, and shot by my face like a
flash;
I swooned to the earth the next moment, and knew nothing
after the crash.

How long I lay there unconscious 'twas impossible for me to
tell;
My stupor was almost a heaven, my waking almost a hell,—
For I then heard the piteous moaning and shrieking of hus-
bands and wives,
And I thought of the day we all shrink from, when I must
account for their lives;
Mothers rushed by me like maniacs, their eyes glaring madly
and wild;
Fathers, losing their courage, gave way to their grief like a
child;
Children searching for parents, I noticed, as by me they sped,
And lips, that could form naught but "Mamma," were calling
for one perhaps dead.

My mind was made up in a moment, the river should hide me
away,
When, under the still burning rafters I suddenly noticed there
lay
A little white hand: she who owned it was doubtless an object
of love

To one whom her loss would drive frantic, tho' she guarded
 him now from above;
I tenderly lifted the rafters and quietly laid them one side;
How little she thought of her journey when she left for this
 dark fatal ride!
I lifted the last log from off her, and while searching for some
 spark of life,
Turned her little face up in the starlight, and recognized—
 Maggie, my wife!

O Lord! thy scourge is a hard one, at a blow thou hast shat-
 tered my pride;
My life will be one endless nightmare, with Maggie away from
 my side.
How often I'd sat down and pictured the scenes in our long,
 happy life;
How I'd strive through all my life time, to build up a home for
 my wife;
How people would envy us always in our cozy and neat little
 nest;
How I should do all of the labor, and Maggie should all the day
 rest;
How one of God's blessings might cheer us, how some day I
 p'raps should be rich;—
But all of my dreams have been shattered, while I laid there
 asleep at the switch!

I fancied I stood on my trial, the jury and judge I could see;
And every eye in the court room was steadily fixed upon me;
And fingers were pointed in scorn, till I felt my face blushing
 blood-red,
And the next thing I heard were the words, "Hanged by the
 neck until dead."
Then I felt myself pulled once again, and my hand caught
 tight hold of a dress,
And I heard, "What's the matter, dear Jim? You've had a bad
 nightmare, I guess!"
And there stood Maggie, my wife, with never a scar from the
 ditch.
I'd been taking a nap in my bed, and had not been "Asleep at
 the switch."

OLIVER WENDELL HOLMES
(1809–1894)

I HAVE FRAMED on a wall the pearly shell of a chambered nautilus, neatly sliced in half to disclose its beautiful spiral. Holmes's famous poem is pasted on the back. No one before or since has written so movingly about this ancient cephalopod whose ancestors go back to the Ordovician period, earlier even than fishes.

This clever little "living fossil" (it almost vanished with the dinosaurs) uses its small tentacles, aided by spurts of water from its head, to swim backward through night seas in search of food. It invented the submarine. By adjusting the amount of seawater in its chambers, it can alter the depth at which it scavenges. Its primitive eye is like a pinhole camera—no lens or eyelids, just an open pupil. In Holmes's day it was thought that the nautilus added a new chamber every year. Recent research shows it can build a new compartment in three to seven months.

"The Chambered Nautilus" appeared in Holmes's *The Autocrat of the Breakfast-Table* after an earlier printing in the *Atlantic Monthly* (February 1858). Holmes originated the poem's metrical form, and always considered it his finest poem. Merle Johnson, in *You Know These Lines!,* quotes Holmes as saying:

> In writing the poem I was filled with a better feeling—the highest state of mental exaltation and the most crystalline clairvoyance, as it seemed to me, that had ever been granted me—I mean that lucid vision of one's thought, and of all forms of expression which will be at once precise and musical, which is the poet's special gift, however large or small in amount or value.

The line about Triton and his wreathed horn is taken, of course, from the last line of Wordsworth's sonnet "The World Is Too Much with Us," the penultimate inclusion in *Best Remembered Poems*. In that book you will also find three of Holmes's better known poems as well as details about his life.

Here is how Holmes, in *The Autocrat,* introduced the poem:

> Did I not say to you a little while ago that the universe swam in an ocean of similitudes and analogies? I will not quote Cowley, or Burns, or Wordsworth just now, to show you what thoughts were suggested to them by the simplest natural objects, such as a flower or a leaf; but I will read you a few lines, if you do not object, suggested by looking at a section of one of those chambered shells to which is given the name of "pearly nautilus." The last will show you the series of enlarging compartments successively dwelt in by the animal that inhabits the shell, which is built in a widening spiral. Can you find no lesson in this?

The Chambered Nautilus

This is the ship of pearl which, poets feign,
 Sails the unshadowed main,—
 The venturous bark that flings
On the sweet summer wind its purpled wings
In gulfs enchanted, where the Siren sings,
 And coral reefs lie bare,
Where the cold sea-maids rise to sun their streaming hair.

Its webs of living gauze no more unfurl;
 Wrecked is the ship of pearl!
 And every chambered cell,
Where its dim dreaming life was wont to dwell,
As the frail tenant shaped his growing shell,
 Before thee lies revealed,—
Its irised ceiling rent, its sunless crypt unsealed!

Year after year beheld the silent toil
 That spread his lustrous coil;
 Still, as the spiral grew,
He left the past year's dwelling for the new,
Stole with soft step its shining archway through,
 Built up its idle door,
Stretched in his last-found home, and knew the old no more.

Thanks for the heavenly message brought by thee,
 Child of the wandering sea,
 Cast from her lap, forlorn!
From thy dead lips a clearer note is born
Than ever Triton blew from wreathed horn!
 While on mine ear it rings,
Through the deep caves of thought I hear a voice that sings:—

Build thee more stately mansions, O my soul.
 As the swift seasons roll!
 Leave thy low-vaulted past!
Let each new temple, nobler than the last,
Shut thee from heaven with a dome more vast,
 Till thou at length art free,
Leaving thine outgrown shell by life's unresting sea!

THOMAS HOOD
(1799–1845)

Hood's "Song of the Shirt" and "Bridge of Sighs" are in *Best Remembered Poems* along with a brief account of his career. "I Remember, I Remember" is another poem by this prolific versifier that was enormously admired in Hood's day.

I Remember, I Remember

I remember, I remember,
 The house where I was born,
The little window where the sun
 Came peeping in at morn:
He never came a wink too soon,
 Nor brought too long a day;
But now, I often wish the night
 Had borne my breath away.

I remember, I remember,
 The roses, red and white;
The violets and the lily-cups,
 Those flowers made of light!
The lilacs where the robin built,
 And where my brother set
The laburnum on his birthday,—
 The tree is living yet!

I remember, I remember,
 Where I was used to swing;
And thought the air must rush as fresh
 To swallows on the wing:
My spirit flew in feathers then,
 That is so heavy now,
And summer pools could hardly cool
 The fever on my brow!

I remember, I remember,
 The fir trees dark and high;
I used to think their slender tops
 Were close against the sky:

It was a childish ignorance,
 But now 'tis little joy
To know I'm farther off from heaven
 Than when I was a boy.

MARY (BOTHAM) HOWITT
(1799–1888)

HOWITT and her husband William were two of the most famous, most prolific writers in nineteenth-century England. Both turned out scores of books—novels, short stories, history, verse, not to mention volumes on which the pair collaborated. Mary Howitt became best known for fiction and poetry written for children, and her translations of works by Hans Christian Andersen and other writers.

The Howitts abandoned their Quaker upbringing to become leaders in England's Spiritualist mania. William became a skilled automatic writer, his hand guided by "departed spirits." He contributed more than a hundred articles to *Spiritual Magazine,* passionately arguing that Spiritualism was in harmony with primitive Christianity, and bashing the doctrine of incarnation. He produced in two volumes *A History of the Supernatural in All Ages and Nations, and in All Churches, Christian and Pagan, Demonstrating a Universal Faith* (1863). Both Howitts settled and died in Rome. A few years before her death, Mary converted to Roman Catholicism.

"The Spider and the Fly" was included in one of Howitt's collections of verse, *Sketches of Natural History* (1834). Apparently it was based on an earlier folk song. I own *The School Reader, Third Book* (New York, 1853), edited by Charles W. Sanders, in which the words of Howitt's poem are set to music by an unnamed composer. Above the song is "Words by C. W. Sanders"! The song's chorus is a couplet that repeats the line: "Will you, will you, will you, will you, walk in, Mrs. Fly?" Lewis Carroll parodied the chorus, as well as the poem's first line and meter, in the song sung by the Mock Turtle in *Alice's Adventures in Wonderland.*

Is there not something sad about the fact that a writer so admired by her contemporaries is remembered today only for a child's poem about a spider and a fly?

I found an amusing poem titled "Another Spider and Fly," by Laura Garland Carr, in *The Children's Speaker* (1897), compiled by John Wesley Hanson, Jr. It tells of a fly who is about to be gobbled by a spider when a swallow swoops down and eats the spider.

The Spider and the Fly

"Will you walk into my parlor?" said the spider to the fly;
"'Tis the prettiest little parlor that ever you did spy.
The way into my parlor is up a winding stair,
And I have many pretty things to show when you are there."
"O no, no," said the little fly, "to ask me is in vain,
For who goes up your winding stair can ne'er come down
 again."

"I'm sure you must be weary, dear, with soaring up so high;
Will you rest upon my little bed?" said the spider to the fly.
"There are pretty curtains drawn around, the sheets are fine
 and thin,
And if you like to rest awhile, I'll snugly tuck you in."
"O no, no," said the little fly, "for I've often heard it said,
They *never, never wake* again, who sleep upon *your* bed."

Said the cunning spider to the fly, "Dear friend, what shall I
 do,
To prove the warm affection I've always felt for you?
I have within my pantry good store of all that's nice;
I'm sure you're very welcome; will you please to take a slice?"
"O no, no," said the little fly, "kind sir, that cannot be;
I've heard what's in your pantry, and I do not wish to see."

"Sweet creature!" said the spider, "you're witty and you're
 wise,
How handsome are your gauzy wings, how brilliant are your
 eyes!
I have a little looking-glass upon my parlor shelf,
If you'll step in one moment, dear, you shall behold yourself."
"I thank you, gentle sir," she said, "for what you're pleased to
 say,
And bidding you good-morning *now*, I'll call *another* day."

The spider turned him round about, and went into his den,
For well he knew the silly fly would soon be back again:
So he wove a subtle web, in a little corner sly,
And set his table ready to dine upon the fly.
Then he came out to his door again, and merrily did sing,
"Come hither, hither, pretty fly, with the pearl and silver wing:
Your robes are green and purple; there's a crest upon your
 head;

Your eyes are like the diamond bright, but mine are dull as
 lead."

Alas, alas! how very soon this silly little fly,
Hearing his wily flattering words, came slowly flitting by.
With buzzing wings she hung aloft, then near and nearer
 drew,
Thinking only of her brilliant eyes, and green and purple hue;
Thinking only of her crested head—*poor foolish thing!* At last,
Up jumped the cunning spider, and fiercely held her fast.
He dragged her up his winding stair, into his dismal den,
Within his little parlor; but she ne'er came out again!

And now, dear little children, who may this story read,
To idle, silly, flattering words, I pray you ne'er give heed;
Unto an evil counselor close heart, and ear, and eye,
And take a lesson from this tale of the Spider and the Fly.

LEIGH HUNT
(1784–1859)

MAD CAREW, in Milton Hayes's ballad about the green eye of the little yellow
god, lost his life trying to please a vain woman. Count de Lorge, in Hunt's
almost forgotten poem, managed to save his skin, but behaved more sensibly
after his heroic act.

Hunt was a London journalist, poet, essayist and political radical. I won't
repeat what I said about him in *Best Remembered Poems,* where I reprinted his
"Abou Ben Adhem" and "Jenny Kiss'd Me." I forgot to add there that when a
grade-school teacher asked Isaac Asimov why Abou's name led all the rest,
Asimov replied, "Because his last name began with A."

The Glove and the Lions

King Francis was a hearty king, and loved a royal sport,
And one day, as his lions fought, sat looking on the court.
The nobles filled the benches, with the ladies in their pride,
And 'mongst them sat the Count de Lorge, with one for whom
 he sighed:
And truly 'twas a gallant thing to see that crowning show,
Valor and love, and a king above, and the royal beasts below.

Ramped and roared the lions, with horrid laughing jaws;
They bit, they glared, gave blows like beams, a wind went with
 their paws;
With wallowing might and stifled roar they rolled on one
 another,
Till all the pit with sand and mane was in a thunderous
 smother;
The bloody foam above the bars came whisking through the
 air;
Said Francis then, "Faith, gentlemen, we're better here than
 there."

De Lorge's love o'erheard the King, a beauteous lively dame,
With smiling lips and sharp bright eyes, which always seemed
 the same;
She thought, The Count my lover is brave as brave can be;
He surely would do wondrous things to show his love of me;
King, ladies, lovers, all look on; the occasion is divine;
I'll drop my glove, to prove his love; great glory will be mine.

She dropped her glove, to prove his love, then looked at him
 and smiled;
He bowed, and in a moment leaped among the lions wild:
The leap was quick, return was quick, he has regained his
 place,
Then threw the glove, but not with love, right in the lady's face.
"By Heaven," said Francis, "rightly done!" and he rose from
 where he sat;
"No love," quoth he, "but vanity, sets love a task like that."

COATES KINNEY
(1826–1904)

I WOULD GUESS that thousands of poems and songs have been written about the sound of rain on the roof. Indeed, when I was a boy I wrote one myself, though happily all I can recall are the banal opening lines:

> I love to listen to the rain
> On the roof and window pane,
> And the moaning of a train
> Somewhere near.

The most famous of such poems in English, "Rain on the Roof," is the only poem remembered out of the total effusions of Coates Kinney. A lawyer and

newspaperman, Kinney was born at Kinney's Corners, New York, but lived most of his life in Ohio. Newspapers he edited included *The Xenia Torchlight, Cincinnati Daily Times, Springfield Daily Republic* and *Ohio State Journal.* He ended his Civil War career as a lieutenant-colonel, and served in the Ohio senate in 1881–1882.

"Rain on the Roof" first appeared in *Our Great West* (September 22, 1849) and later in Kinney's privately published *Keeuka and Other Poems* (1855). *Lyrics of the Ideal and the Real,* and *Mists of Fire and Some Eclogues* were two later collections of his undistinguished verse.

Slason Thompson, in his collection *The Humbler Poets* (1885), prints a final stanza of this poem as revised by the author. He considers it inferior to the original, commenting that "poets are proverbially unsafe revisers of their own work." Here is the altered stanza:

> Art hath nought of tone or cadence
> That can work with such a spell
> In the soul's mysterious fountains,
> Whence the tears of rapture well,
> As that melody of Nature,
> That subdued, subduing strain,
> Which is played upon the shingles
> By the patter of the rain.

Rain on the Roof

When the humid shadows hover
 Over all the starry spheres,
And the melancholy darkness
 Gently weeps in rainy tears,
What a joy to press the pillow
 Of a cottage-chamber bed,
And to listen to the patter
 Of the soft rain overhead!

Every tinkle on the shingles
 Has an echo in the heart;
And a thousand dreamy fancies
 Into busy being start,
And a thousand recollections
 Weave their bright hues into woof,
As I listen to the patter
 Of the rain upon the roof.

Now in fancy comes my mother,
 As she used to, years agone,

To survey her darling dreamers,
　Ere she left them till the dawn;
Oh! I see her bending o'er me,
　As I list to this refrain
Which is played upon the shingles
　By the patter of the rain.

Then my little seraph sister,
　With her wings and waving hair,
And her bright-eyed cherub brother—
　A serene, angelic pair!—
Glide around my wakeful pillow,
　With their praise or mild reproof,
As I listen to the murmur
　Of the soft rain on the roof.

And another comes to thrill me
　With her eye's delicious blue;
And forget I, gazing on her,
　That her heart was all untrue:
I remember but to love her
　With a rapture kin to pain,
And my heart's quick pulses vibrate
　To the patter of the rain.

There is naught in Art's bravuras,
　That can work with such a spell
In the spirit's pure, deep fountains,
　Whence the holy passions well,
As that melody of Nature,
　That subdued, subduing strain
Which is played upon the shingles
　By the patter of the rain.

WILLIAM KNOX
(1789–1825)

WILLIAM KNOX was a Scottish farmer, educated at the University of Edinburgh, who gave up farming to become a writer. Of his many poems, only "Oh! Why Should the Spirit of Mortal Be Proud?" has survived. I have been able to learn little about him except that he was a lovable alcoholic, much admired by Sir Walter Scott, and died in poverty at age 36.

Lincoln clipped Knox's one memorable poem from a newspaper, where it ran without a byline, and for many years was unable to find out who wrote it. It was his favorite poem. He memorized all its stanzas and loved to recite them to friends and guests. I do not know where it was first published, or whether it is included in Knox's *The Lonely Heart and Other Poems* (1825).

The poem appeared as a small book in 1865, and again in 1876 (with many later editions), profusely illustrated by L. B. Humphrey.

Oh! Why Should the Spirit of Mortal Be Proud?

Oh! why should the spirit of mortal be proud?
Like a swift-fleeting meteor, a fast-flying cloud,
A flash of the lightning, a break of the wave,
Man passeth from life to his rest in the grave.

The leaves of the oak and the willow shall fade,
Be scattered around, and together be laid;
And the young and the old, and the low and the high
Shall moulder to dust and together shall die.

The infant a mother attended and loved;
The mother that infant's affection who proved;
The husband that mother and infant have blessed,—
Each, all, are away to their dwellings of rest.

The maid on whose cheek, on whose brow, in whose eye,
Shone beauty and pleasure—her triumphs are by;
And the memory of those who loved her and praised
Are alike from the minds of the living erased.

The hand of the king that the sceptre hath borne;
The brow of the priest that the mitre hath worn,
The eye of the sage, and the heart of the brave,
Are hidden and lost in the depth of the grave.

The peasant whose lot was to sow and to reap;
The herdsman who climbed with his goats up the steep;
The beggar who wandered in search of his bread,
Have faded away like the grass that we tread.

The saint who enjoyed the communion of heaven;
The sinner who dared to remain unforgiven;
The wise and the foolish, the guilty and just,
Have quietly mingled their bones in the dust.

So the multitude goes, like the flowers or the weed
That withers away to let others succeed;
So the multitude comes, even those we behold,
To repeat every tale that has often been told.

For we are the same our fathers have been;
We see the same sights our fathers have seen;
We drink the same stream, and view the same sun,
And run the same course our fathers have run.

The thoughts we are thinking our fathers would think;
From the death we are shrinking our fathers would shrink;
To the life we are clinging they also would cling;
But it speeds for us all, like a bird on the wing.

They loved, but the story we cannot unfold;
They scorned, but the heart of the haughty is cold;
They grieved, but no wail from their slumbers will come;
They joyed, but the tongue of their gladness is dumb.

They died, aye! they died: and we things that are now,
Who walk on the turf that lies over their brow,
Who make in their dwelling a transient abode,
Meet the things that they met on their pilgrimage road.

Yea! hope and despondency, pleasure and pain,
We mingle together in sunshine and rain;
And the smiles and the tears, the song and the dirge,
Still follow each other, like surge upon surge.

'Tis the wink of an eye, 'tis the draught of a breath,
From the blossom of health to the paleness of death,
From the gilded saloon to the bier and the shroud,
Oh! why should the spirit of mortal be proud?

HENRY WADSWORTH LONGFELLOW
(1807–1882)

I WILL NOT repeat here what I had to say in *Best Remembered Poems* about America's most loved poet throughout most of the previous century. In that anthology I included nine of Longfellow's poems that I thought were the most familiar today. Presented here are two less remembered ones, but favorites in Longfellow's time.

Clocks have long been symbols of the inexorable passage of time. Will we live again in eternity, or vanish forever? The old clock doesn't say.

Longfellow based his poem on an eloquent passage in the writings of Jacques Bridaine, a French Catholic priest. It describes the ticking of a clock as repeating *"Toujours, jamais! Jamais, toujours!"* The poem's first book appearance was in *The Belfry of Bruges and Other Poems* (1845). "The Rainy Day" was included in *Ballads and Other Poems* (1841), and was set to music in 1847 by Isaac Baker Woodbury.

The Old Clock on the Stairs

Somewhat back from the village street
Stands the old-fashioned country-seat.
Across its antique portico
Tall poplar-trees their shadows throw;
And from its station in the hall
An ancient timepiece says to all,—
 "Forever—never!
 Never—forever!"

Half-way up the stairs it stands,
And points and beckons with its hands
From its case of massive oak,
Like a monk, who, under his cloak,
Crosses himself, and sighs, alas!
With sorrowful voice to all who pass,—
 "Forever—never!
 Never—forever!"

By day its voice is low and light;
But in the silent dead of night,
Distinct as a passing footstep's fall,
It echoes along the vacant hall,
Along the ceiling, along the floor,
And seems to say, at each chamber-door,—
 "Forever—never!
 Never—forever!"

Through days of sorrow and of mirth,
Through days of death and days of birth,
Through every swift vicissitude
Of changeful time, unchanged it has stood,

And as if, like God, it all things saw,
It calmly repeats those words of awe,—
 "Forever—never!
 Never—forever!"

In that mansion used to be
Free-hearted Hospitality;
His great fires up the chimney roared;
The stranger feasted at his board;
But, like the skeleton at the feast,
That warning timepiece never ceased,—
 "Forever—never!
 Never—forever!"

There groups of merry children played,
There youths and maidens dreaming strayed;
O precious hours! O golden prime,
And affluence of love and time!
Even as a miser counts his gold,
Those hours the ancient timepiece told,—
 "Forever—never!
 Never—forever!"

From that chamber, clothed in white,
The bride came forth on her wedding night;
There, in that silent room below,
The dead lay in his shroud of snow;
And in the hush that followed the prayer,
Was heard the old clock on the stair,—
 "Forever—never!
 Never—forever!"

All are scattered now and fled,
Some are married, some are dead;
And when I ask, with throbs of pain,
"Ah! when shall they all meet again?"
As in the days long since gone by,
The ancient timepiece makes reply,—
 "Forever—never!
 Never—forever!"

Never here, forever there,
Where all parting, pain, and care,
And death, and time shall disappear,—

Forever there, but never here!
The horologe of Eternity
Sayeth this incessantly,—
 "Forever—never!
 Never—forever!"

The Rainy Day

The day is cold, and dark, and dreary;
It rains, and the wind is never weary;
The vine still clings to the mouldering wall,
But at every gust the dead leaves fall,
 And the day is dark and dreary.

My life is cold, and dark, and dreary;
It rains, and the wind is never weary;
My thoughts still cling to the mouldering Past,
But the hopes of youth fall thick in the blast,
 And the days are dark and dreary.

Be still, sad heart! and cease repining;
Behind the clouds is the sun still shining;
Thy fate is the common fate of all,
Into each life some rain must fall,
 Some days must be dark and dreary.

JOHN LUCKEY McCREERY
(1835–1906)

JOHN McCREERY was born in Sweden, New York, the son of a Methodist
minister. His career in journalism took him to Delhi, Iowa, in 1857, where he
bought a weekly newspaper that he edited until the end of the Civil War. After
working for newspapers in Dubuque, he became a clerk with the Committee
on Indian Affairs, Washington, D.C., where he later held other government
jobs.

"There Is No Death," in ten stanzas, first appeared, with McCreery's byline,
in *Arthur's Home Journal* 22 (July 1863): 41. Then a funny thing happened. A
newspaper reprinted the poem, crediting it to one "E. Bulmer," probably a
fictitious name. Other editors assumed that "Bulmer" was a wrong spelling of
"Bulwer," which they took to be Edward Robert Lytton Bulwer, England's poet
who used the pen name Owen Meredith!

McCreery's poem was soon reprinted everywhere—in anthologies, newspapers, magazines, hymnbooks and school readers—as the work of Meredith. Even Burton Stevenson, who devotes a chapter to all this in *Famous Single Poems*, credited the poem to Meredith in his earlier *Home Book of Verse*.

No other poem was more recited at funerals and burial sites than "There Is No Death." Poor McCreery spent the rest of his life struggling vainly to prove the poem was indeed his. He included it as the first poem in *Songs of Toil and Triumph* (1883), where he revised it heavily, and expanded it to sixteen stanzas. Stevenson considers the revised version "vastly inferior" to the original, and finds little merit in any of the other poems in the book.

McCreery died in Duluth, Minnesota, after an appendicitis operation, and was buried in Glenwood Cemetery, in the nation's capital. The first stanza of his once-admired poem is on his modest tombstone.

There Is No Death

There is no death! The stars go down
 To rise upon some other shore,
And bright in heaven's jeweled crown
 They shine for evermore.

There is no death! The dust we tread
 Shall change beneath the summer showers
To golden grain or mellow fruit
 Or rainbow-tinted flowers.

The granite rocks disorganize
 To feed the hungry moss they bear;
The forest leaves drink daily life
 From out the viewless air.

There is no death! The leaves may fall,
 The flowers may fade and pass away—
They only wait, through wintry hours,
 The coming of the May.

There is no death! An angel form
 Walks o'er the earth with silent tread;
He bears our best-loved things away,
 And then we call them "dead."

He leaves our hearts all desolate—
 He plucks our fairest, sweetest flowers;
Transplanted into bliss, they now
 Adorn immortal bowers.

The bird-like voice, whose joyous tones
 Made glad this scene of sin and strife,
Sings now an everlasting song
 Amid the tree of life.

Where'er He sees a smile too bright,
 Or soul too pure for taint of vice,
He bears it to that world of light,
 To dwell in Paradise.

Born unto that undying life,
 They leave us but to come again;
With joy we welcome them—the same
 Except in sin and pain.

And ever near us, though unseen,
 The dear immortal spirits tread;
For all the boundless universe
 Is Life—there are no dead!

There Is No Death [Revised version]

There is no death! The stars go down
 To rise upon some other shore,
And bright in heaven's jewelled crown
 They shine forevermore.

There is no death! The forest leaves
 Convert to life the viewless air;
The rocks disorganize to feed
 The hungry moss they bear.

There is no death! The dust we tread
 Shall change, beneath the summer showers
To golden grain, or mellowed fruit,
 Or rainbow-tinted flowers.

There is no death! The leaves may fall,
 And flowers may fade and pass away—
They only wait, through wintry hours,
 The warm, sweet breath of May.

There is no death! The choicest gifts
 That heaven hath kindly lent to earth

Are ever first to seek again
　The country of their birth.

And all things that for growth or joy
　Are worthy of our love or care,
Whose loss has left us desolate,
　Are safely garnered there.

Though life become a desert waste,
　We know its fairest, sweetest flowers,
Transplanted into Paradise,
　Adorn immortal bowers.

The voice of birdlike melody
　That we have missed and mourned so long,
Now mingles with the angel choir
　In everlasting song.

There is no death! Although we grieve
　When beautiful, familiar forms
That we have learned to love are torn
　From our embracing arms—

Although with bowed and breaking heart,
　With sable garb and silent tread,
We bear their senseless dust to rest,
　And say that they are "dead,"

They are not dead! They have but passed
　Beyond the mists that blind us here
Into the new and larger life
　Of that serener sphere.

They have but dropped their robe of clay
　To put their shining raiment on;
They have not wandered far away—
　They are not "lost" nor "gone."

Though disenthralled and glorified
　They still are here and love us yet;
The dear ones they have left behind
　They never can forget.

And sometimes, when our hearts grow faint
　Amid temptations fierce and deep,
Or when the wildly raging waves
　Of grief or passion sweep,

We feel upon our fevered brow
 Their gentle touch, their breath of balm;
Their arms enfold us, and our hearts
 Grow comforted and calm.

And ever near us, though unseen,
 The dear, immortal spirits tread—
For all the boundless universe
 Is Life—there are no dead!

JOHN BOYLE O'REILLY
(1844–1890)

OF ALL THE poets mentioned in this book, O'Reilly had the most flamboyant and most tragic life. Irish-born, he became an ardent Fenian, a member of the secret organization dedicated to ending British rule in Ireland. He enlisted in the Tenth Hussars, a British cavalry regiment, for the purpose of winning the troops over to the Fenian cause. When his sedition was discovered, he was court-martialed and ordered shot. After this sentence was commuted to twenty years, he was "transported" to a penal colony in Bunbury, Australia.

Three years later O'Reilly escaped on an American whaling ship. As *American Authors 1600–1900* puts it, "after hair-trigger escapes and breathless adventures" he finally reached Philadelphia. A devout Roman Catholic, he settled in Boston where he edited *The Pilot*, a Catholic newspaper, until he died at age 45 from a sleeping-pill overdose. In 1876 he had organized an expedition to Australia that rescued all the Irish political prisoners sent there from England.

O'Reilly's novel *Moondyne* drew on his experiences as a convict in Australia. His books of verse include *Songs from Southern Seas* and *Songs, Legends, and Ballads*. Only "The Cry of the Dreamer" has survived.

It was in Boston that artists and writers first began to call themselves "bohemians." O'Reilly's "In Bohemia," hailed as this subculture's national anthem, was his most often recited poem. It begins and ends with "I'd rather live in Bohemia than in any other land." A biography of the poet by J. J. Roche has an introduction by Cardinal James Cardinal Gibbons, and a monument to O'Reilly stands in Boston.

The Cry of the Dreamer

I am tired of planning and toiling
 In the crowded hives of men,
Heart-weary of building and spoiling,

And spoiling and building again,
And I long for the dear old river,
　Where I dreamed my youth away;
For a dreamer lives forever,
　And a toiler dies in a day.

I am sick of the showy seeming,
　Of life that is half a lie;
Of the faces lined with scheming
　In the throng that hurries by;
From the sleepless thought's endeavor
　I would go where the children play;
For a dreamer lives forever,
　And a thinker dies in a day.

I can feel no pride, but pity,
　For the burdens the rich endure;
There is nothing sweet in the city
　But the patient lives of the poor.
Oh, the little hands too skillful,
　And the child-mind choked with weeds!
The daughter's heart grown willful
　And the father's heart that bleeds!

No! no! from the street's rude bustle,
　From trophies of mart and stage,
I would fly to the wood's low rustle
　And the meadows' kindly page.
Let me dream as of old by the river,
　And be loved for my dreams alway;
For a dreamer lives forever,
　And the toiler dies in a day.

EDWARD E. ("TED") PARAMORE, JR.
(1895–1956)

THIS WILL BE a long introduction, partly because Paramore is not covered in the usual references on American writers, and also because his life was as bizarre as Yukon Jake's.

Born in Manchester, Massachusetts, he attended the Hill School in Pottstown, Pennsylvania, and later was voted the most brilliant and versatile man in Yale's class of 1917. His first job was that of newspaper reporter covering the

Russian Revolution in Petrograd. He is said to have guided a trainload of American refugees safely through Siberia. Later he became the old *New York World*'s drama critic. The *New York Times* obituary (May 2, 1956, page 31), my sole source for Paramore's life, quoted a paragraph from what it said was a *Times* story about him in 1927. (I was unable to locate this in the *Times* 1927 yearbook index.) Here is the paragraph:

> [Paramore] also has been a sailor before the mast. He was run out of town in Santa Ynez, because he dropped three flies in a baseball game; put in jail in Nicaragua during revolutionary troubles, from which place he escaped within two hours after his incarceration, and fired by Hal Roach for insubordination at Culver City, Calif.

Paramore contributed to several leading magazines during the twenties, and was on the masthead of *Time*'s first issue as a "weekly contributor." Somehow he got to Hollywood to become one of its most successful screen-writers. During the thirties he produced scripts for many films, including *The Thundering Herd, The Bitter Tea of General Yen, Baby Take a Bow, The Farmer Takes a Wife* and *The Virginian*.

Paramore collaborated with his old friend F. Scott Fitzgerald on the 1938 screen adaptation of Erich Maria Remarque's popular novel *Three Comrades*. The film starred Margaret Sullavan. Sharp disagreements over the script are vividly detailed in Fitzgerald's letter to "Ted" (October 24, 1937)—a letter included in *The Letters of F. Scott Fitzgerald* (1969), edited by Andrew Turnbull.

Paramore also wrote several plays. His three-act mystery melodrama *Set a Thief* ran on Broadway in 1926, and was published the following year by Samuel French. *Ringside* was on Broadway in 1928. *Mr. Peebles and Mr. Hooker* closed after a four-day run in 1946.

In 1956 Paramore and his wife were returning to their home in Santa Barbara, California, from a vacation in New York City. During a stopover at Shreveport, Louisiana, he fell in a parking garage, and failed to recover from a badly fractured skull. The *Times* obituary said he was "about 60," and called him "a poet, playwright, journalist and adventurer." It seems likely he wrote other poems than his famous ballad about Jake, but if so, I have failed to locate any.

Paramore's marvelous parody of Robert Service first appeared in *Vanity Fair* (August 1921) and was reprinted three times by the same magazine. A small book, *The Ballad of Yukon Jake*, illustrated by "Hogarth, Jr." (pseudonym of a young Rockwell Kent), was published by Coward McCann in 1928. Paramore is said to have collected five thousand dollars from Mack Sennett for having borrowed from the ballad for his silent comedy *Yukon Jake*.

The reference to "Tecla pearl" in the ninth stanza had me puzzled until English professor William Harmon found "tecla" defined in *The Oxford English Dictionary* as a proprietary name, trademarked in 1908, for a variety of artificial pearl. Evelyn Waugh's novel *Vile Bodies* (1930), Chapter 6, speaks of "heirlooms of priceless value . . . among Tecla pearls."

The Ballad of Yukon Jake

Oh, the North Countree is a hard countree
That mothers a bloody brood;
And its icy arms hold hidden charms
For the greedy, the sinful and lewd.
And strong men rust, from the gold and the lust
That sears the Northland soul,
But the wickedest born, from the Pole to the Horn,
Is the Hermit of Shark Tooth Shoal.

Now Jacob Kaime was the Hermit's name,
In the days of his pious youth,
Ere he cast a smirch on the Baptist Church
By betraying a girl named Ruth.
But now men quake at "Yukon Jake,"
The Hermit of Shark Tooth Shoal,
For that is the name that Jacob Kaime
Is known by from Nome to the Pole.
He was just a boy and the parson's joy
(Ere he fell for the gold and the muck),
And had learned to pray, with the hogs and the hay
On a farm near Keokuk.

But a Service tale of illicit kale—
And whiskey and women wild—
Drained the morals clean as a soup-tureen
From this poor but honest child.
He longed for the bite of a Yukon night
And the Northern Light's weird flicker,
Or a game of stud in the frozen mud,
And the taste of raw red licker.
He wanted to mush along in the slush,
With a team of huskie hounds,
And to fire his gat at a beaver hat
And knock it out of bounds.

So he left his home for the hell-town Nome,
On Alaska's ice-ribbed shores,
And he learned to curse and to drink, and worse—
Till the rum dripped from his pores,
When the boys on a spree were drinking it free
In a Malamute saloon

And Dan Megrew and his dangerous crew
Shot craps with the piebald coon;
When the Kid on his stool banged away like a fool
At a jag-time melody,
And the barkeep vowed, to the hardboiled crowd,
That he'd cree-mate Sam McGee—

Then Jacob Kaime, who had taken the name
Of Yukon Jake, the Killer,
Would rake the dive with his forty-five
Till the atmosphere grew chiller.
With a sharp command he'd make 'em stand
And deliver their hard-earned dust,
Then drink the bar dry, of rum and rye,
As a Klondike bully must.
Without coming to blows he would tweak the nose
Of Dangerous Dan Megrew,
And becoming bolder, throw over his shoulder
The lady that's known as Lou.

Oh, tough as a steak was Yukon Jake—
Hardboiled as a picnic egg.
He washed his shirt in the Klondike dirt,
And drank his rum by the keg.
In fear of their lives (or because of their wives)
He was shunned by the best of his pals,
An outcast he, from the comraderie
Of all but wild animals.
So he bought him the whole of Shark Tooth Shoal,
A reef in the Bering Sea,
And he lived by himself on a sea lion's shelf
In lonely iniquity.

But, miles away, in Keokuk, Ia.,
Did a ruined maiden fight
To remove the smirch from the Baptist Church
By bringing the heathen Light.
And the Elders declared that all would be squared
If she carried the holy words
From her Keokuk home to the hell-town Nome
To save those sinful birds.
So, two weeks later, she took a freighter,
For the gold-cursed land near the Pole,

But Heaven ain't made for a lass that's betrayed—
She was wrecked on Shark Tooth Shoal!

All hands were tossed in the Sea, and lost—
All but the maiden Ruth,
Who swam to the edge of the sea lion's ledge
Where abode the love of her youth.
He was hunting a seal for his evening meal
(He handled a mean harpoon)
When he saw at his feet, not something to eat,
But a girl in a frozen swoon,
Whom he dragged to his lair by her dripping hair,
And he rubbed her knees with gin.
To his great surprise, she opened her eyes
And revealed—his Original Sin!

His eight-months beard grew stiff and weird
And it felt like a chestnut burr,
And he swore by his gizzard—and the Arctic blizzard,
That he'd do right by her.
But the cold sweat froze on the end of her nose
Till it gleamed like a Tecla pearl,
While her bright hair fell, like a flame from hell,
Down the back of the grateful girl.
But a hopeless rake was Yukon Jake
The Hermit of Shark Tooth Shoal!
And the dizzy maid he rebetrayed
And wrecked her immortal soul! . . .

Then he rowed her ashore, with a broken oar,
And he sold her to Dan Megrew
For a huskie dog and some hot egg-nog—
As rascals are wont to do.
Now ruthless Ruth is a maid uncouth
With scarlet cheeks and lips,
And she sings rough songs to the drunken throngs
That come from the sealing ships.
For a rouge-stained kiss from this infamous miss
They will give a seal's sleek fur,
Or perhaps a sable, if they are able;
It's much the same to her.

Oh, the North Countree is a rough countree,
That mothers a bloody brood;

And its icy arms hold hidden charms
For the greedy, the sinful and lewd.
And strong men rust, from the gold and the lust
That sears the Northland soul,
But the wickedest born from the Pole to the Horn
Was the Hermit of Shark Tooth Shoal!

SAMUEL MINTURN PECK
(1854–1938)

PECK IS ANOTHER example of a once-admired writer of verse, songs, essays, novels and short stories who was never taken seriously by critics. Born in Tuscaloosa, where he spent his entire life, Peck served in the Alabama state legislature and was designated the state's first poet laureate.

Books of Peck's verse include *Caps and Bells* (1886), *Rings and Love Knots* (1892), *Rhymes and Roses* (1895), *Maybloom and Myrtle* (1910) and *The Autumn Trail* (1925). I have no idea in what book his most popular poem, "A Kiss in the Rain," can be found, or where it was first published.

A Kiss in the Rain

One stormy night I chanced to meet
 A lassie in the town;
Her locks were like the ripened wheat,
 Her laughing eyes were brown.
I watched her as she tripped along,
 Till madness filled my brain,
And then—and then I know 'twas wrong—
 I kissed her in the rain.

With rain-drops shining on her cheek,
 Like dewdrops on a rose,
The little lassie strove to speak,
 My boldness to oppose;
She strove in vain, and, quivering,
 Her fingers stole in mine;
And then the birds began to sing
 The sun began to shine.

Oh, let the clouds grow dark above,
 My heart is light below;

'Tis always summer when we love,
 However winds may blow;
And I am proud as any prince,
 All honors I disdain;
She says I am her rain-beau, since
 I kissed her in the rain.

NORA PERRY
(1841–1896)

BORN IN DUDLEY, Massachusetts, and brought up in Providence, Rhode Island, Perry moved to Boston where she was a correspondent for several out-of-town newspapers before she began to earn a living by writing stories for girls. Her verse is collected in several volumes. A sentimental sixteen-stanza poem about Marge and Madge, titled "After the Ball," was her most popular poem, but "The Love-Knot" made its way into more anthologies.

The Love-Knot

Tying her bonnet under her chin,
She tied her raven ringlets in;
But not alone in the silken snare
Did she catch her lovely floating hair,
For, tying her bonnet under her chin,
She tied a young man's heart within.

They were strolling together up the hill,
Where the wind came blowing merry and chill;
And it blew the curls, a frolicsome race,
All over the happy peach-colored face.
Till, scolding and laughing, she tied them in,
Under her beautiful, dimpled chin.

And it blew a color, bright as the bloom
Of the pinkest fuchsia's tossing plume,
All over the cheeks of the prettiest girl
That ever imprisoned a romping curl,
Or, in tying her bonnet under her chin,
Tied a young man's heart within.

Steeper and steeper grew the hill,
Madder, merrier, chillier still

The western wind blew down, and played
The wildest tricks with the little maid,
As, tying her bonnet under her chin,
She tied a young man's heart within.

O western wind, do you think it was fair
To play such tricks with her floating hair?
To gladly, gleefully, do your best
To blow her against the young man's breast,
Where he as gladly folded her in,
And kissed her mouth and her dimpled chin?

Ah! Ellery Vane, you little thought,
An hour ago, when you besought
This country lass to walk with you,
After the sun had dried the dew,
What terrible danger you'd be in,
As she tied her bonnet under her chin!

EDGAR ALLAN POE
(1809–1849)

IN *BEST REMEMBERED POEMS* I included Poe's "Annabel Lee," "The Raven,"
"To Helen" and "The Bells." Less well known today is *A Dream within a Dream,*
which I regard as Poe's finest, most moving lyric.

Here is the poem's history as given in a footnote in *Edgar Allan Poe,* a book
begun by Margaret Allerton and completed by Hardin Craig (1935):

> This poem is protean in form. It was first published as "Imitation"
> in the 1827 volume; in a widely differing version entitled "To — —
> —" in the 1829 volume; appended to "Tamerlane" in the 1831
> collection; and in the greatly altered form given in this text in the
> *Flag of Our Union,* March 31, 1849. At the time of his death, Poe was
> preparing to publish the poem again with still further slight revisions
> in the *Examiner* of Richmond (Whitty, *Complete Poems,* viii–ix). The
> interesting feature of the history of the poem is the fact that Poe
> continued to meditate on the theme of the transitoriness of his life.
> In the earliest version life has been like a dream, and he is willing to
> let it pass. Into the 1829 form comes the figure of the sands sifting
> through his fingers; life seems paltry, but he will endure it. Into the
> latest versions comes the conclusion that life is like a dream within a
> dream. The poem grows less and less autobiographical.

The three volumes referred to are Poe's *Tamerlane and Other Poems* (1827),
Al Aaraaf, Tamerlane, and Minor Poems (1829) and *Poems* (1831).

A Dream within a Dream

Take this kiss upon the brow!
And, in parting from you now,
Thus much let me avow:
You are not wrong, who deem
That my days have been a dream;
Yet if Hope has flown away
In a night, or in a day,
In a vision, or in none,
Is it therefore the less *gone?*
All that we see or seem
Is but a dream within a dream.

I stand amid the roar
Of a surf-tormented shore,
And I hold within my hand
Grains of the golden sand—
How few! yet how they creep
Through my fingers to the deep,
While I weep—while I weep!
O God! can I not grasp
Them with a tighter clasp?
O God! can I not save
One from the pitiless wave?
Is *all* that we see or seem
But a dream within a dream?

JAMES WHITCOMB RILEY
(1849–1916)

NOTES ON RILEY'S life are given in *Best Remembered Poems* as an introduction to four of his most popular poems. Here we reprint another of his famous poems. It first ran in the *Indianapolis Journal* (June 14, 1884), and made its first book appearance in *Afterwhiles* (1888).

"Out to Old Aunt Mary's" was set to music in 1897 by R. Atkinson, and later by others. It was one of Riley's most effective stage recitations. On one occasion, when the actress Ellen Terry was in the audience, she was visibly overcome with emotion.

Out to Old Aunt Mary's

Wasn't it pleasant, O brother mine,
In those old days of the lost sunshine
 Of youth—when the Saturday's chores were through,
 And the "Sunday's wood" in the kitchen, too,
 And we went visiting, "me and you,"
 Out to Old Aunt Mary's?—

"Me and you"—And the morning fair,
With the dewdrops twinkling everywhere;
 The scent of the cherry-blossoms blown
 After us, in the roadway lone,
 Our capering shadows onward thrown—
 Out to Old Aunt Mary's!

It all comes back so clear to-day!
Though I am as bald as you are gray,—
 Out by the barn-lot and down the lane
 We patter along in the dust again,
 As light as the tips of the drops of the rain,
 Out to Old Aunt Mary's.

The few last houses of the town;
Then on, up the high creek-bluffs and down;
 Past the squat toll-gate, with its well-sweep pole,
 The bridge, and "the old 'babtizin'-hole,' "
 Loitering, awed, o'er pool and shoal,
 Out to Old Aunt Mary's.

We cross the pasture, and through the wood,
Where the old gray snag of the poplar stood,
 Where the hammering "red-heads" hopped awry,
 And the buzzard "raised" in the "clearing"-sky
 And lolled and circled, as we went by
 Out to Old Aunt Mary's.

Or, stayed by the glint of the redbird's wings,
Or the glitter of song that the bluebird sings,
 All hushed we feign to strike strange trails,
 As the "big braves" do in the Indian tales,
 Till again our real quest lags and fails—
 Out to Old Aunt Mary's.—

And the woodland echoes with yells of mirth
That make old war-whoops of minor worth! . . .
 Where such heroes of war as we?—
 With bows and arrows of fantasy,
 Chasing each other from tree to tree
 Out to Old Aunt Mary's!

And then in the dust of the road again;
And the teams we met, and the countrymen;
 And the long highway, with sunshine spread
 As thick as butter on country bread,
 Our cares behind, and our hearts ahead
 Out to Old Aunt Mary's.—

For only, now, at the road's next bend
To the right we could make out the gable-end
 Of the fine old Huston homestead—not
 Half a mile from the sacred spot
 Where dwelt our Saint in her simple cot—
 Out to Old Aunt Mary's.

Why, I see her now in the open door
Where the little gourds grew up the sides and o'er
 The clapboard roof!—And her face—ah, me!
 Wasn't it good for a boy to see—
 And wasn't it good for a boy to be
 Out to Old Aunt Mary's?—

The jelly—the jam and the marmalade,
And the cherry and quince "preserves" she made!
 And the sweet-sour pickles of peach and pear,
 With cinnamon in 'em, and all things rare!—
 And the more we ate was the more to spare,
 Out to Old Aunt Mary's!

Ah! was there, ever, so kind a face
And gentle as hers, or such a grace
 Of welcoming, as she cut the cake
 Or the juicy pies that she joyed to make
 Just for the visiting children's sake—
 Out to Old Aunt Mary's!

The honey, too, in its amber comb
One only finds in an old farm-home;

And the coffee, fragrant and sweet, and ho!
So hot that we gloried to drink it so,
 With spangles of tears in our eyes, you know—
 Out to Old Aunt Mary's.

And the romps we took, in our glad unrest!—
Was it the lawn that we loved the best,
 With its swooping swing in the locust trees,
 Or was it the grove, with its leafy breeze,
 Or the dim haymow, with its fragrancies—
 Out to Old Aunt Mary's.

Far fields, bottom-lands, creek-banks—all,
We ranged at will.—Where the waterfall
 Laughed all day as it slowly poured
 Over the dam by the old mill-ford,
 While the tail-race writhed, and the mill-wheel roared—
 Out to Old Aunt Mary's.

But home, with Aunty in nearer call,
That was the best place, after all!—
 The talks on the back porch, in the low
 Slanting sun and the evening glow,
 With the voice of counsel that touched us so,
 Out to Old Aunt Mary's.

And then, in the garden—near the side
Where the beehives were and the path was wide,—
 The apple-house—like a fairy cell—
 With the little square door we knew so well,
 And the wealth inside but our tongues could tell—
 Out to Old Aunt Mary's.

And the old spring-house, in the cool green gloom
Of the willow trees,—and the cooler room
 Where the swinging shelves and the crocks were kept,
 Where the cream in a golden languor slept,
 While the waters gurgled and laughed and wept—
 Out to Old Aunt Mary's.

And as many a time have you and I—
Barefoot boys in the days gone by—
 Knelt, and in tremulous ecstasies
 Dipped our lips into sweets like these,—
 Memory now is on her knees
 Out to Old Aunt Mary's.—

For, O my brother so far away,
This is to tell you—she waits *to-day*
 To welcome us:—Aunt Mary fell
 Asleep this morning, whispering, "Tell
 The boys to come." . . . And all is well
 Out to Old Aunt Mary's.

EPES SARGENT
(1813–1880)

AFTER SERVING on the staff of several Boston papers, Sargent moved to Manhattan where he also worked for newspapers and edited his own short-lived *Sargent's New Monthly Magazine.* Back in Boston, he became editor of the *Transcript* before retiring to write romantic novels, plays, popular school textbooks and spellers, and to edit "speakers." He also edited a six-volume edition of the poems of Thomas Hood.

Sargent's most admired poem—it was set to music by Henry Russell—was "A Life on the Ocean Wave." It ran first in the New York *Mirror* (May 19, 1838) under the pseudonym of "Zeta," and was included in *Songs of the Sea* (1847), one of Sargent's many books of verse.

In his elderly years Sargent became one of the nation's most gullible Spiritualists, wasting his talents on such now forgotten works as *Planchette, the Despair of Science; The Proof Palpable of Immortality;* and *The Scientific Basis of Spiritualism.*

A Life on the Ocean Wave

A life on the ocean wave,
 A home on the rolling deep,
Where the scattered waters rave,
 And the winds their revels keep!
Like an eagle caged, I pine
 On this dull, unchanging shore:
Oh! give me the flashing brine,
 The spray and the tempest's roar!

Once more on the deck I stand
 Of my own swift-gliding craft:
Set sail! farewell to the land!
 The gale follows fair abaft.
We shoot through the sparkling foam

Like an ocean-bird set free;—
　Like the ocean-bird, our home
　　We'll find far out on the sea.

The land is no longer in view,
　The clouds have begun to frown;
But with a stout vessel and crew,
　We'll say, Let the storm come down!
And the song of our hearts shall be,
　While the winds and the waters rave,
A home on the rolling sea!
　A life on the ocean wave!

JOHN GODFREY SAXE
(1816–1887)

SAXE WAS ONE of the most prolific and most admired poets of the nineteenth century. He is best remembered today for his verse about the blind men who examine an elephant, reprinted in my *Best Remembered Poems*.

Our forebears also chuckled over "The Puzzled Census-Taker," which appeared in scores of early anthologies. "Rhyme of the Rail" is perhaps the most admired poem ever written about the pleasures of train travel. Ironically, as I mentioned in *Best Remembered Poems*, Saxe never fully recovered from a severe injury suffered in a train wreck.

The Puzzled Census-Taker

"Got any boys?" the marshal said
　To a lady from over the Rhine;
And the lady shook her flaxen head,
　And civilly answered, *"Nein!"*

"Got any girls?" the marshal said
　To the lady from over the Rhine;
And again the lady shook her head,
　And civilly answered, *"Nein!"*

"But some are dead?" the marshal said
　To the lady from over the Rhine;
And again the lady shook her head,
　And civilly answered, *"Nein!"*

"Husband, of course," the marshal said
 To the lady from over the Rhine;
And again she shook her flaxen head,
 And civilly answered, *"Nein!"*

"The devil you have!" the marshal said
 To the lady from over the Rhine;
And again she shook her flaxen head,
 And civilly answered, *"Nein!"*

"Now, what do you mean by shaking your head,
 And always answering 'Nine?' "
"Ich kann nicht Englisch!" civilly said
 The lady from over the Rhine.

Rhyme of the Rail

Singing through the forests,
 Rattling over ridges,
Shooting under arches,
 Rumbling over bridges,
Whizzing through the mountains,
 Buzzing o'er the vale,—
Bless me! this is pleasant,
 Riding on the Rail!

Men of different "stations"
 In the eye of Fame
Here are very quickly
 Coming to the same.
High and lowly people,
 Birds of every feather,
On a common level
 Traveling together!

Gentleman in shorts,
 Looming very tall;
Gentleman at large,
 Talking very small;
Gentleman in tights,
 With a loose-ish mien;
Gentleman in gray,
 Looking rather green.

Gentleman quite old,
 Asking for the news;
Gentleman in black,
 In a fit of blues;
Gentleman in claret,
 Sober as a vicar;
Gentleman in Tweed,
 Dreadfully in liquor!

Stranger on the right,
 Looking very sunny,
Obviously reading
 Something rather funny.
Now the smiles are thicker,
 Wonder what they mean?
Faith he 's got the KNICKER-
 BOCKER Magazine!

Stranger on the left,
 Closing up his peepers;
Now he snores amain,
 Like the Seven Sleepers;
At his feet a volume
 Gives the explanation,
How the man grew stupid
 From "Association"!

Ancient maiden lady
 Anxiously remarks,
That there must be peril
 'Mong so many sparks!
Roguish-looking fellow,
 Turning to the stranger,
Says it's his opinion
 She is out of danger!

Woman with her baby,
 Sitting *vis à-vis;*
Baby keeps a squalling;
 Woman looks at me;
Asks about the distance,
 Says it 's tiresome talking,
Noises of the cars
 Are so very shocking!

Market-woman careful
 Of the precious casket,
Knowing eggs are eggs,
 Tightly holds her basket;
Feeling that a smash,
 If it came, would surely
Send her eggs to pot
 Rather prematurely!

Singing through the forests,
 Rattling over ridges,
Shooting under arches,
 Rumbling over bridges,
Whizzing through the mountains,
 Buzzing o'er the vale,—
Bless me! this is pleasant,
 Riding on the Rail!

ROBERT SERVICE
(1874–1958)

SERVICE'S TWO MOST famous poems, "The Shooting of Dan McGrew" and "The Cremation of Sam McGee," are included in *Best Remembered Poems,* which also includes information on Service's life.

"The Spell of the Yukon" was another of his earliest and most admired poems. It appeared in his first book of verse, *Songs of a Sourdough,* published in England in 1907, and in the U.S. that same year as *The Spell of the Yukon and Other Verses.* The popularity of his poetry has never waned.

The Spell of the Yukon

I wanted the gold, and I sought it;
 I scrabbled and mucked like a slave.
Was it famine or scurvy—I fought it;
 I hurled my youth into a grave.
I wanted the gold, and I got it—
 Came out with a fortune last fall,—
Yet somehow life's not what I thought it,
 And somehow the gold isn't all.

No! There's the land. (Have you seen it?)
 It's the cussedest land that I know,
From the big, dizzy mountains that screen it
 To the deep, deathlike valleys below.
Some say God was tired when He made it;
 Some say it's a fine land to shun;
Maybe; but there's some as would trade it
 For no land on earth—and I'm one.

You come to get rich (damned good reason);
 You feel like an exile at first;
You hate it like hell for a season,
 And then you are worse than the worst.
It grips you like some kinds of sinning;
 It twists you from foe to a friend;
It seems it's been since the beginning;
 It seems it will be to the end.

I've stood in some mighty-mouthed hollow
 That's plumb-full of hush to the brim;
I've watched the big, husky sun wallow
 In crimson and gold, and grow dim,
Till the moon set the pearly peaks gleaming,
 And the stars tumbled out, neck and crop;
And I've thought that I surely was dreaming,
 With the peace o' the world piled on top.

The summer—no sweeter was ever;
 The sunshiny woods all athrill;
The grayling aleap in the river,
 The bighorn asleep on the hill.
The strong life that never knows harness;
 The wilds where the caribou call;
The freshness, the freedom, the farness—
 O God! how I'm stuck on it all.

The winter! the brightness that blinds you,
 The white land locked tight as a drum,
The cold fear that follows and finds you,
 The silence that bludgeons you dumb.
The snows that are older than history,
 The woods where the weird shadows slant;
The stillness, the moonlight, the mystery,
 I've bade 'em good-by—but I can't.

There's a land where the mountains are nameless,
 And the rivers all run God knows where;
There are lives that are erring and aimless,
 And deaths that just hang by a hair;
There are hardships that nobody reckons;
 There are valleys unpeopled and still;
There's a land—oh, it beckons and beckons,
 And I want to go back—and I will.

They're making my money diminish;
 I'm sick of the taste of champagne.
Thank God! when I'm skinned to a finish
 I'll pike to the Yukon again.
I'll fight—and you bet it's no sham-fight;
 It's hell!—but I've been there before;
And it's better than this by a damsite—
 So me for the Yukon once more.

There's gold, and it's haunting and haunting;
 It's luring me on as of old;
Yet it isn't the gold that I'm wanting
 So much as just finding the gold.
It's the great, big, broad land 'way up yonder,
 It's the forests where silence has lease;
It's the beauty that thrills me with wonder,
 It's the stillness that fills me with peace.

EDWARD ROWLAND SILL
(1841–1887)

SILL WAS BORN in Windsor, Connecticut, and graduated from Yale. Harvard's Divinity School turned him into a lifelong agnostic. He was a professor of English literature at the University of California from 1874 to 1882.

Books of poems by Sill are *The Heritage and Other Poems* (1868), *Venus of Milo and Other Poems* (1883) and two posthumous works, *Hermione and Other Poems* (1889) and *Poems of Edward Rowland Sill* (1902). Many of his poems were contributed to magazines under the name of Andrew Hedbrooke.

Sill was an intimate friend of the Harvard philosopher Josiah Royce. In *The Spirit of Modern Philosophy* Royce quotes "The Fool's Prayer" in its entirety, on which he comments:

> As I knew him, the poet of these verses was peculiarly sensitive to the presence in the world of that willfulness both of fortune and of our fellows, which not because of conscious sinfulness, nor yet

because of any obviously necessary discord of motives, but because of
mere brute accident or stupidity, tears to pieces whatever is spiritual,
kills our infant children, leaves our unrecognized heroes to die
neglected and ineffective, sunders the wounded hearts of faithful
lovers, makes brother war with brother, plunges society into bitter
confusions, defeats over and over the most sacred ideals.

Included here are the only two of Sill's poems that survive in anthologies. I
have no idea where they were first published.

The Fool's Prayer

The royal feast was done; the King
 Sought some new sport to banish care,
And to his jester cried: "Sir Fool,
 Kneel now, and make for us a prayer!"

The jester doffed his cap and bells,
 And stood the mocking court before;
They could not see the bitter smile
 Behind the painted grin he wore.

He bowed his head, and bent his knee
 Upon the monarch's silken stool;
His pleading voice arose: "O Lord,
 Be merciful to me, a fool!

"No pity, Lord, could change the heart
 From red with wrong to white as wool;
The rod must heal the sin: but, Lord,
 Be merciful to me, a fool!

" 'Tis not by guilt the onward sweep
 Of truth and right, O Lord, we stay;
'Tis by our follies that so long
 We hold the earth from heaven away.

"These clumsy feet, still in the mire,
 Go crushing blossoms without end;
These hard, well-meaning hands we thrust
 Among the heart-strings of a friend.

"The ill-timed truth we might have kept—
 Who knows how sharp it pierced and stung?
The word we had not sense to say—
 Who knows how grandly it had rung?

"Our faults no tenderness should ask,
 The chastening stripes must cleanse them all;
But for our blunders—oh, in shame
 Before the eyes of heaven we fall.

"Earth bears no balsam for mistakes;
 Men crown the knave, and scourge the tool
That did his will; but Thou, O Lord,
 Be merciful to me, a fool!"

The room was hushed; in silence rose
 The King, and sought his gardens cool,
And walked apart, and murmured low,
 "Be merciful to me, a fool!"

Opportunity

This I beheld, or dreamed it in a dream:—
There spread a cloud of dust along a plain;
And underneath the cloud, or in it, raged
A furious battle, and men yelled, and swords
Shocked upon swords and shields. A prince's banner
Wavered, then staggered backward, hemmed by foes.

A craven hung along the battle's edge,
And thought, "Had I a sword of keener steel—
That blue blade that the king's son bears—but this
Blunt thing!"—he snapped and flung it from his hand,
And lowering crept away and left the field.

Then came the king's son, wounded, sore bestead,
And weaponless, and saw the broken sword,
Hilt-buried in the dry and trodden sand,
And ran and snatched it, and with battle-shout
Lifted afresh he hewed his enemy down,
And saved a great cause that heroic day.

ARABELLA EUGENIE SMITH
(1844–1916)

BELLE SMITH, as she liked to be called, is another of Burton Stevenson's "one-poem poets." "If I Should Die To-night" not only is her only published poem, but so far as anyone knows, she never wrote another. Born in Litchfield, Ohio, she was taken by her parents to Iowa, where she taught in public schools. Later she was a librarian and instructor at her alma mater, Tabor College, in Hillsboro, Kansas. She became librarian of the Newton, Iowa, public library. Little else is known about her.

Smith's famous poem was published in the *Christian Union* (June 18, 1873) over the initials "B. S." After someone set it to music, it quickly became a favorite among singers and reciters at country fairs and church socials. Because it was widely printed anonymously, or credited to others, several false claimants popped out of the woodwork.

Chief among the claimants was Irvine Dungan, a prominent attorney and politician in Jackson, Ohio. Confronted with evidence of the poem's publication in 1873, he "laughed heartily," as one newspaper put it, and said he had recited the poem as early as 1867 in the town's courthouse. Investigation showed there was no courthouse in 1867, the building having burned down seven years earlier.

Benjamin Franklin King (1857–1894), who signed his light verse "Ben King," is another one-time poet. Sadly, his only claim to fame rests on a parody of Smith's poem.

If I Should Die To-night

If I should die to-night,
My friends would look upon my quiet face
Before they laid it in its resting-place,
And deem that death had left it almost fair;
And, laying snow-white flowers against my hair,
Would smooth it down with tearful tenderness,
And fold my hands with lingering caress,—
Poor hands, so empty and so cold to-night!

If I should die to-night,
My friends would call to mind with loving thought
Some kindly deed the icy hands had wrought,
Some gentle word the frozen lips had said,
Errands on which the willing feet had sped;
The memory of my selfishness and pride,
My hasty words would all be put aside,
And so I should be loved and mourned to-night.

If I should die to-night,
Even hearts estranged would turn once more to me,
Recalling other days remorsefully;
The eyes that chill me with averted glance
Would look upon me as of yore, perchance,
And soften in the old familiar way,
For who could war with dumb, unconscious clay?
So I might rest, forgiven of all to-night.

Oh, friends! I pray to-night,
Keep not your kisses for my dead, cold brow:
The way is lonely, let me feel them now.
Think gently of me; I am travelworn;
My faltering feet are pierced with many a thorn.
Forgive, oh, hearts estranged, forgive, I plead!
When dreamless rest is mine I shall not need
The tenderness for which I long to-night.

If I Should Die To-night (by Ben King)

If I should die to-night,
And you should come to my cold corpse and say,
Weeping and heartsick o'er my lifeless clay—
If I should die to-night,
And you should come in deepest grief and woe—
And say: "Here's that ten dollars that I owe,"
I might arise in my large white cravat
And say, "What's that?"

If I should die to-night,
And you should come to my cold corpse and kneel,
Clasping my bier to show the grief you feel,
I say, if I should die to-night,
And you should come to me, and there and then
Just even hint at paying me that ten,
I might arise the while,
But I'd drop dead again.

FRANK LEBBY STANTON
(1857–1927)

BORN IN CHARLESTON, South Carolina, Stanton settled in Atlanta where he wrote a popular column, "Just from Georgia," for *The Atlanta Constitution*. His patriotic, inspirational, sentimental verse was collected in books with such titles as *Songs of the Soil, Comes One with a Song, Songs from Dixie Land, Up From Georgia* and *Little Folks Down South*.

I have here selected his best-recalled inspirational poem and a lyric that became famous when Ethelbert Nevin, in 1901, set it to music. It is easy to remember a popular song, but who bothers to learn who wrote the words or the melody? I do not know where these two poems were first printed, or in what books they were first included.

If you are interested in popular verse of the "Keep a-Goin" sort, I recommend the anthology *It Can Be Done: Poems of Inspiration,* edited by Joseph Morris and St. Clair Adams (1921). My copy is a thirty-first printing. A companion volume by the same authors, *Facing Forward: Poems of Courage,* followed in 1925.

Keep a-Goin!

If you strike a thorn or rose,
 Keep a-goin!
If it hails or if it snows,
 Keep a-goin!
'Taint no use to sit an' whine
When the fish ain't on your line;
Bait your hook an' keep a-tryin'—
 Keep a-goin!

When the weather kills your crop,
 Keep a-goin!
Though 'tis work to reach the top,
 Keep a-goin!
S'pose you're out o' ev'ry dime,
Gittin' broke ain't any crime;
Tell the world you're feelin' *prime*—
 Keep a-goin!

When it looks like all is up,
 Keep a-goin!
Drain the sweetness from the cup,
 Keep a-goin!

See the wild birds on the wing,
Hear the bells that sweetly ring,
When you feel like singin', sing—
 Keep a-goin'!

Sweetes' Li'l' Feller

Sweetes' li'l' feller,
 Everybody knows;
Dunno what to call him,
 But he mighty lak' a rose!
Lookin' at his Mammy
 Wid eyes so shiny blue,
Mek' you think that heav'n
 Is comin' clost ter you!
W'en he's dar a-sleepin',
 In his li'l' place,
Think I see de angels
 Lookin' through de place.
W'en de dark is fallin',
 W'en de shadders creep,
Den dey comes on tiptoe
 Ter kiss 'im in his sleep.
Sweetes' li'l' feller,
 Everybody knows;
Dunno what to call 'im,
 But he mighty lak' a rose!
Lookin' at his Mammy
 Wid eyes so shiny blue,
Mek' you think that heav'n
 Is comin' clost ter you!

GEORGE WASHINGTON STEVENS
(1866–1926)

THIS AMUSING TRIBUTE to church organists is by a Utica (New York)-born man who worked a few years on the staff of the Toledo *Times* before becoming director of the Toledo Museum of Art, a post he held until his death.

Stevens's books of poetry include *The King and the Harper and Other Poems*

and *Things.* I haven't checked them to find out whether the organist is male or female in Stevens's original version. Hazel Felleman, in her *Best Loved Poems of the American People,* has him a man, but in *The Speaker's Garland* 10, no. 38 (1914), the organist is a woman.

The Organist

I wonder how the organist
 Can do so many things;
He's getting ready long before
 The choir stands up and sings;
He's pressing buttons, pushing stops,
 He's pulling here and there,
And testing all the working parts
 While listening to the prayer.

He runs a mighty big machine,
 It's full of funny things;
A mass of boxes, pipes and tubes
 And sticks and slats and strings;
There's little whistles for a cent
 In rows and rows and rows;
I'll bet there's twenty miles of tubes
 As large as garden hose.

There's scores as large as stovepipes and
 There's lots so big and wide
That several little boys I know
 Could play around inside.
From little bits of piccolos
 That hardly make a toot
There's every size up to the great
 Big elevator chute.

The organist knows every one
 And how they ought to go;
He makes them rumble like a storm,
 Or plays them sweet and low;
At times you think them very near;
 At times they're soaring high,
Like angel voices, singing far
 Off, somewhere in the sky.

For he can take this structure, that's
　As big as any house,
And make it squeak as softly as
　A tiny little mouse;
And then he'll jerk out something with
　A movement of the hand,
And make you think you're listening to
　A military band.

He plays it with his fingers and
　He plays it with his toes,
And if he really wanted to
　He'd play it with his nose;
He's sliding up and down the bench,
　He's working with his knees;
He's dancing round with both his feet
　As lively as you please.

I always like to take a seat
　Where I can see him go;
He's better than a sermon, and
　He does me good, I know;
I like the life and movement and
　I like to hear him play;
He is the most exciting thing
　In town on Sabbath day.

WILLIAM LEROY STIDGER
(1885–1949)

REVEREND STIDGER, born in Moundsville, West Virginia, was one of the nation's most influential Methodist ministers, serving as pastor of churches in San Francisco, Detroit and other cities. He was a popular radio preacher and poet, and author of a syndicated newspaper column titled "How to Get the Most Out of Life." Among his dozens of books, mostly about religion, were biographies of Henry Ford and the poet Edwin Markham.

"I Saw God Wash the World" is the title poem of a 1934 volume, one of his several books of verse. Although *Granger's Index to Poetry* lists sixteen of his poems, you won't find him mentioned in any major reference on twentieth-century authors.

I Saw God Wash the World

I saw God wash the world last night
 With his sweet showers on high,
And then, when morning came, I saw
 Him hang it out to dry.

He washed each tiny blade of grass
 And every trembling tree;
He flung his showers against the hill,
 And swept the billowing sea.

The white rose is a cleaner white,
 The red rose is more red,
Since God washed every fragrant face
 And put them all to bed.

There's not a bird, there's not a bee
 That wings along the way
But is a cleaner bird and bee
 Than it was yesterday.

I saw God wash the world last night.
 Ah, would He had washed me
As clean of all my dust and dirt
 As that old white birch tree.

CARLYLE FAHLSWORTH STRAUB
(1898–1950)

I FIRST CAME across this gutsy lyric in a 1918 anthology titled *Songs of Men*, edited by Robert Frothingham. In the foreword he calls the poem "an anonymous bit of verse written especially for this anthology by one of our best-known poets." The poem turns up in later anthologies, always with the byline "unknown."

I was surprised to encounter the poem in a 1927 book, *Songs of a Sinner*, by Carlyle Fahlsworth Straub. An acknowledgment page thanks twenty-eight magazines and newspapers for allowing poems to be reprinted. In his book Straub retitles his poem "The God of Grit," and alters it much for the worse. The first line is replaced by "I sing of the God with the craw of grit." "Snatch a friend," several lines later, becomes "save a friend"; "Swallow the pill" is now "Swallow the last," and "Tell a pal" is "tell a friend." The entire final stanza of eight lines has given way to a pallid couplet:

So I sing my song to the God of Grit;
The tolerant God who'll never quit.

And now for a small enigma which perhaps a reader can solve. The birth and death dates for Straub, given above, are based on the assumption that he is the Carlyle Fahlsworth Straub who was arrested in New York City in 1950 for swindling a printer out of $550 for falsely claiming he had been authorized to write a book about horse racing. According to a story in the *New York Times* (January 26, 1950, page 50), Straub was a "society bootlegger" who had eight previous arrests. In 1944 he had been sentenced to 2½ years in Sing Sing for swindling Cartier jewelers. He claimed to have once studied professional dancing under the famous Vernon Castle. A brief obituary in the *New York Times* (February 25, 1950, page 30) reported his death (no cause given) in Bellevue Hospital before his case came to court. His age was 52.

No mention is made in either story of Straub having written poetry. It seems impossible that two New Yorkers would have the same unusual name of Carlyle Fahlsworth Straub, yet it seems equally unlikely that the author of the poems in *Songs of a Sinner* could be a criminal.

If Straub the poet was indeed Straub the sinner, who beat a jail sentence by dying in midwinter, the following lyric from his book of verse would have made an appropriate epitaph:

Birth.
A day of joy,
A day of sorrow.
Friends today,
Foes tomorrow.
Clouds without a silver lining,
Sweetness of a summer's breath,
Castles wrecked;
Love repining;
Winter's cold—
Death.

The Little Red God

Here 's a little red song to the god of guts,
Who dwells in palaces, brothels, huts;
The little Red God with the craw of grit;
The god who never learned how to quit;
He is neither a fool with a frozen smile,
Or a sad old toad in a cask of bile;
He can dance with a shoe-nail in his heel
And never a sign of his pain reveal;
He can hold a mob with an empty gun
And turn a tragedy into fun;
Kill a man in a flash, a breath,

Or snatch a friend from the claws of death;
Swallow the pill of assured defeat
And plan attack in his slow retreat;
Spin the wheel till the numbers dance,
And bite his thumb at the god of Chance;
Drink straight water with whisky-soaks,
Or call for liquor with temperance folks;
Tearless stand at the graven stone,
Yet weep in the silence of night, alone;
Worship a sweet, white virgin's glove,
Or teach a courtesan how to love;
Dare the dullness of fireside bliss,
Or stake his soul for a wanton's kiss;
Blind his soul to a woman's eyes
When she says she loves and he knows she lies;
Shovel dung in the city mart
To earn a crust for his chosen art;
Build where the builders all have failed,
And sail the seas that no man has sailed;
Run a tunnel or dam a stream,
Or damn the men who financed the dream;
Tell a pal what his work is worth,
Though he lose his last, best friend on earth;
Lend the critical monkey-elf
A razor—hoping he 'll kill himself;
Wear the garments he likes to wear,
Never dreaming that people stare;
Go to church if his conscience wills,
Or find his own—in the far, blue hills.

He is kind and gentle, or harsh and gruff;
He is tender as love—or he 's rawhide tough;
A rough-necked rider in spurs and chaps,
Or well-groomed son of the town—perhaps;
And this is the little Red God I sing,
Who cares not a wallop for anything
That walks or gallops, that crawls or struts,
No matter how clothed—if it has n't guts.

JANE TAYLOR

(1783–1824)

JANE TAYLOR IS best remembered today for her lyric that begins "Twinkle, twinkle, little star," which I included in *Best Remembered Poems* along with information about her life. She and her sister Ann wrote many poems more widely read and quoted in their day than "The Star."

"The Philosopher's Scales," here offered, was one of Taylor's poems that can be found in dozens of nineteenth-century collections of popular verse.

When Burton Stevenson included the poem in his *Home Book of Verse,* he left out the eighth stanza—perhaps because he didn't know who Howard was—as well as the moralizing stanza at the end. (John Howard [1726–1790] was a British philanthropist and penal reformer.)

The Philosopher's Scales

A monk, when his rites sacerdotal were o'er,
In the depths of his cell with its stone-covered floor,
Resigning to thought his chimerical brain,
Once formed the contrivance we now shall explain;
But whether by magic's or alchemy's powers
We know not; indeed, 'tis no business of ours.

Perhaps it was only by patience and care,
At last, that he brought his invention to bear.
In youth 'twas projected, but years stole away,
And ere 'twas complete he was wrinkled and gray;
But success is secure, unless energy fails;
And at length he produced the Philosopher's Scales.

"What were they?" you ask. You shall presently see;
These scales were not made to weigh sugar and tea.
Oh no; for such properties wondrous had they,
That qualities, feelings, and thoughts they could weigh,
Together with articles small or immense,
From mountains or planets to atoms of sense.

Naught was there so bulky but there it would lay,
And naught so ethereal but there it would stay,
And naught so reluctant but in it must go:
All which some examples more clearly will show.

The first thing he weighed was the head of Voltaire,
Which retained all the wit that had ever been there;
As a weight, he threw in the torn scrap of a leaf
Containing the prayer of the penitent thief;
When the skull rose aloft with so sudden a spell
That it bounced like a ball on the roof of the cell.

One time he put in Alexander the Great,
With the garment that Dorcas had made, for a weight;
And though clad in armor from sandals to crown,
The hero rose up and the garment went down.

A long row of almshouses, amply endowed
By a well-esteemed Pharisee, busy and proud,
Next loaded one scale; while the other was pressed
By those mites the poor widow dropped into the chest:
Up flew the endowment, not weighing an ounce,
And down, down the farthing-worth came with a bounce.

Again, he performed an experiment rare;
A monk, with austerities bleeding and bare,
Climbed into his scale; in the other was laid
The heart of our Howard, now partly decayed;
When he found, with surprise, that the whole of his brother
Weighed less, by some pounds, than this bit of the other.

By further experiments (no matter how)
He found that ten chariots weighed less than one plough;
A sword with gilt trappings rose up in the scale,
Though balanced by only a ten-penny nail;
A shield and a helmet, a buckler and spear,
Weighed less than a widow's uncrystallized tear.

A lord and a lady went up at full sail,
When a bee chanced to light on the opposite scale;
Ten doctors, ten lawyers, two courtiers, one earl,
Ten counsellors' wigs, full of powder and curl,
All heaped in one balance and swinging from thence,
Weighed less than a few grains of candor and sense;
A first-water diamond, with brilliants begirt,
Than one good potato just washed from the dirt;
Yet not mountains of silver and gold could suffice
One pearl to outweigh,—'twas the Pearl of Great Price.

Last of all, the whole world was bowled in at the grate,
With the soul of a beggar to serve for a weight,

When the former sprang up with so strong a rebuff
That it made a vast rent and escaped at the roof!
When balanced in air, it ascended on high,
And sailed up aloft, a balloon in the sky;
While the scale with the soul in't so mightily fell
That it jerked the philosopher out of his cell.

MORAL.

Dear reader, if e'er self-deception prevails,
We pray you to try *The Philosopher's Scales:*
But if they are lost in the ruins around,
Perhaps a good substitute thus may be found:—
Let *judgment* and *conscience in circles be cut,*
To which strings of thought may be carefully put:
Let these be made even with caution extreme,
And *impartiality* use for a beam:
Then bring those good actions which pride overrates,
And tear up your *motives* to serve for the weights.

CHARLES HANSON TOWNE
(1877–1949)

BORN IN LOUISVILLE, Kentucky, Towne lived in Manhattan where, in spite of only one year at City College, he became one of the city's top magazine editors. At various times he edited *The Designer, The Smart Set, McClure's* and *Harper's Bazaar.* He played the clergyman in *Life with Father,* a Broadway success, in 1940–1941.

Towne wrote several novels—*Tinsel* was the best received—several plays and many books of nonfiction. His poems were collected in numerous books and in *Selected Poems* (1925). The poem that follows is the only one for which he is remembered.

The Best Road of All

I like a road that leads away to prospects white and fair,
A road that is an ordered road, like a nun's evening prayer;
But best of all I love a road that leads to God knows where.

You come upon it suddenly—you cannot seek it out;
It's like a secret still unheard and never noised about;
But when you see it, gone at once is every lurking doubt.

It winds beside some rushing stream where aspens lightly
 quiver;
It follows many a broken field by many a shining river;
It seems to lead you on and on, forever and forever.

You tramp along its dusty way beneath the shadowy trees,
And hear beside you chattering birds or happy booming bees,
And all around you golden sounds, the green leaves' litanies.

And here's a hedge and there's a cot; and then, strange,
 sudden turns—
A dip, a rise, a little glimpse where the red sunset burns;
A bit of sky at evening time, the scent of hidden ferns.

A winding road, a loitering road, the finger mark of God,
Traced when the Maker of the world leaned over ways untrod.
See! Here He smiled His glowing smile, and lo, the golden-
 rod!

I like a road that wanders straight; the king's highway is fair,
And lovely are the sheltered lanes that take you here and
 there;
But best of all I love a road that leads to God knows where.

JOHN TOWNSEND TROWBRIDGE
(1827–1916)

BORN IN OGDEN, New York, Townsend was a self-educated journalist and writer
who settled in the Boston area after serving as an editor on several periodicals.
He became famous for his novels for boys, some forty of them, many appearing
first in *The Youth's Companion* and *Our Young Folks* under the pseudonym Paul
Crayton. Trowbridge also was a prolific writer of verse, his *Collected Poems*
appearing in 1903.

No one reads Trowbridge's fiction today, and his only remembered poem is
"Darius Green and His Flying-Machine." It first ran in *Our Young Folks* (March
1867). A special book edition, illustrated by Wallace Goldsmith, was published
in 1910 with a brief foreword by R. L. S. (Robert Louis Stevenson?).

The poem also was included in *The Vagabonds and Other Poems* (1869). The
title poem was the most famous of all Trowbridge's poems in his day. It is a
fourteen-stanza ballad about an alcoholic beggar who drifts along the roads

with a fiddle and his dog Roger. The man playing the fiddle and his dog
performing tricks, the two vagabonds are able barely to get by on food, booze
and a place to sleep. He recalls his happier days and a lost love, and longs for
death.

Hayward Cirker has called my attention to the similarity of the endings of
this poem and "Casey at the Bat." "It is paradoxical," he writes, "that Ameri-
can society, so driven and obsessed by success, would enjoy two poems that end
with abject failure."

Darius Green and His Flying-Machine

If ever there lived a Yankee lad,
Wise or otherwise, good or bad,
Who, seeing the birds fly, did n't jump
With flapping arms from stake or stump,
 Or, spreading the tail
 Of his coat for a sail,
Take a soaring leap from post or rail,
 And wonder why
 He could n't fly,
And flap and flutter and wish and try,—
If ever you knew a country dunce
Who did n't try that as often as once,
All I can say is, that 's a sign
He never would do for a hero of mine.

An aspiring genius was D. Green:
The son of a farmer,—age fourteen;
His body was long and lank and lean,—
Just right for flying, as will be seen;
He had two eyes, each bright as a bean,
And a freckled nose that grew between,
A little awry,—for I must mention
That he had riveted his attention
Upon his wonderful invention,
Twisting his tongue as he twisted the strings,
Working his face as he worked the wings,
And with every turn of gimlet and screw
Turning and screwing his mouth round
 Till his nose seemed bent
 To catch the scent,
Around some corner, of new-baked pies,

And his wrinkled cheeks and his squinting eyes
Grew puckered into a queer grimace,
That made him look very droll in the face,
 And also very wise.
And wise he must have been, to do more
Than ever a genius did before,
Excepting Dædalus of yore
And his son Icarus, who wore
 Upon their backs
 Those wings of wax
He had read of in the old almanacs.
Darius was clearly of the opinion,
That the air is also man's dominion,
And that, with paddle or fin or pinion,
 We soon or late
 Shall navigate
The azure as now we sail the sea.
The thing looks simple enough to me;
 And if you doubt it,
Hear how Darius reasoned about it.

 "Birds can fly,
 An' why can't I?
 Must we give in,"
 Says he with a grin,
 " 'T the bluebird an' phœbe
 Are smarter'n we be?
Jest fold our hands an' see the swaller,
An' blackbird an' catbird beat us holler?
Doos the leetle chatterin', sassy wren,
No bigger'n my thumb, know more than men?
 Jest show me that!
 Er prove 't the bat
Hez got more brains than 's in my hat,
An' I 'll back down, an' not till then!"

He argued further: "Ner I can't see
What 's th' use o' wings to a bumble-bee,
Fer to git a livin' with, more 'n to me;—
 Ain't my business
 Important 's his'n is?

 "That Icarus
 Was a silly cuss,—

Him an' his daddy Dædalus.
They might 'a' knowed wings made o' wax
Would n't stan' sun-heat an' hard whacks.
 I 'll make mine o' luther,
 Er suthin' er other."

And he said to himself, as he tinkered and planned:
"But I ain't goin' to show my hand
To nummies that never can understand
The fust idee that 's big an' grand.
 They 'd 'a' laft an' made fun
O' Creation itself afore 't was done!"
So he kept his secret from all the rest,
Safely buttoned within his vest;
And in the loft above the shed
But vainly they mounted each other's backs,
And poked through knot-holes and pried through cracks;
With wood from the pile and straw from the stacks
He plugged the knot-holes and calked the cracks;
And a bucket of water, which one would think
He had brought up into the loft to drink
 When he chanced to be dry,
 Stood always nigh,
 For Darius was sly!
And whenever at work he happened to spy
At chink or crevice a blinking eye,
He let a dipper of water fly.

"Take that! an' ef ever ye git a peep,
Guess ye 'll ketch a weasel asleep!"
 And he sings as he locks
 His big strong box:—

SONG

"The weasel's head is small an' trim,
An' he is leetle an' long an' slim,
An' quick of motion an' nimble of limb,
 An' ef yeou 'll be
 Advised by me,
Keep wide awake when ye 're ketchin' him!"

 So day after day
He stitched and tinkered and hammered away,
 Till at last 't was done,—

The greatest invention under the sun!
"An' now," says Darius, "hooray fer some fun!"

'T was the Fourth of July,
And the weather was dry,
And not a cloud was on all the sky,
Save a few light fleeces, which here and there,
Half mist, half air,
Like foam on the ocean went floating by:
Just as lovely a morning as ever was seen
For a nice little trip in a flying-machine.

Thought cunning Darius: "Now I sha n't go
Along 'ith the fellers to see the show.
I 'll say I 've got sich a terrible cough!
An' then, when the folks 'ave all gone off,
I 'll hev full swing
Fer to try the thing
An' practyse a leetle on the wing."

"Ain't goin' to see the celebration?"
Says Brother Nate. "No; botheration!
I 've got sich a cold—a toothache—I—
My gracious!—feel 's though I should fly!"

Said Jotham, " 'Sho!
Guess ye better go."
But Darius said, "No!
Should n't wonder 'f yeou might see me, though,
'Long 'bout noon, ef I git red
O' this jumpin', thumpin' pain 'n my head!"
For all the while to himself he said:—

"I tell ye what!
I 'll fly a few times around the lot,
To see how 't seems, then soon 's I 've got
The hang o' the thing, ez likely 's not,
I 'll astonish the nation,
An' all creation,
By flyin' over the celebration!
Over their heads I 'll sail like an eagle;
I 'll balance myself on my wings like a sea-gull;
I 'll dance on the chimbleys; I 'll stan' on the steeple;
I 'll flop up to winders an' scare the people!
I 'll light on the libbe'ty-pole, an' crow;

An' I 'll say to the gawpin' fools below,
　　'What world 's this 'ere
　　That I 've come near?'
Fer I 'll make 'em b'lieve I 'm a chap f'm the moon!
An' I 'll try a race 'ith their ol' bulloon."

　　He crept from his bed;
And, seeing the others were gone, he said,
"I 'm a gittin' over the cold 'n my head."
　　And away he sped,
To open the wonderful box in the shed.

His brothers had walked but a little way
When Jotham to Nathan chanced to say,
"What on airth is he up to, hey?"
"Don'o',—the' 's suthin' er other to pay,
Er he would n't 'a' stayed to hum to-day."

Says Burke, "His toothache 's all in his eye!
He never 'd miss a Fo'th-o'-July,
Ef he hed n't got some machine to try."
Then Sol, the little one, spoke: "By darn!
Le's hurry back an' hide 'n the barn,
An' pay him fer tellin' us that yarn!"
"Agreed!" Through the orchard they creep back,
Along by the fences, behind the stack,
And one by one, through a hole in the wall,
In under the dusty barn they crawl,
Dressed in their Sunday garments all;
And a very astonishing sight was that,
When each in his cobwebbed coat and hat
Came up through the floor like an ancient rat.
　　And there they hid;
　　And Reuben slid
The fastenings back, and the door undid.
　　"Keep dark!" said he,
While I squint an' see what the' is to see."
As knights of old put on their mail,—
　　From head to foot
　　An iron suit,
Iron jacket and iron boot,
Iron breeches, and on the head
No hat, but an iron pot instead,
　　And under the chin the bail,—

I believe they called the thing a helm;
And the lid they carried they called a shield;
And, thus accoutred, they took the field,
Sallying forth to overwhelm
The dragons and pagans that plagued the realm:—
 So this modern knight
 Prepared for flight,
Put on his wings and strapped them tight;
Jointed and jaunty, strong and light;
Buckled them fast to shoulder and hip,—
Ten feet they measured from tip to tip!
And a helm had he, but that he wore,
Not on his head like those of yore,
 But more like the helm of a ship.

 "Hush!" Reuben said,
 "He 's up in the shed!
He 's opened the winder,—I see his head!
 He stretches it out,
 An' pokes it about,
Lookin' to see 'f the coast is clear,
 An' nobody near;—
Guess he don'o' who 's hid in here!
He 's riggin' a spring-board over the sill!
Stop laffin', Solomon! Burke, keep still!
He 's a climbin' out now—Of all the things!
What 's he got on? I van, it 's wings!
An' t' other thing? I vum, it 's a tail!
An' there he sets like a hawk on a rail!
Steppin' careful, he travels the length
Of his spring-board, and teeters to try its strength.
Now he stretches his wings, like a monstrous bat;
Peeks over his shoulder, this way an' that,
Fer to see 'f the' 's any one passin' by;
But the' 's on'y a ca'f an' a goslin' nigh.
They turn up at him a wonderin' eye,
To see— The dragon! he 's goin' to fly!
Away he goes! Jimminy! what a jump!
 Flop—flop—an' plump
 To the ground with a thump!
Flutt'rin' an' flound'rin', all 'n a lump!"

As a demon is hurled by an angel's spear,
Heels over head, to his proper sphere,—

Heels over head, and head over heels,
Dizzily down the abyss he wheels,—
So fell Darius. Upon his crown,
In the midst of the barnyard, he came down,
In a wonderful whirl of tangled strings,
Broken braces and broken springs,
Broken tail and broken wings,
Shooting-stars, and various things!
Away with a bellow fled the calf,
And what was that? Did the gosling laugh?
 'T is a merry roar
 From the old barn-door,
And he hears the voice of Jotham crying,
"Say, D'rius! how de yeou like flyin'?"

Slowly, ruefully, where he lay,
Darius just turned and looked that way,
As he stanched his sorrowful nose with his cuff.
"Wal, I like flyin' well enough,"
He said; "but the' ain't sich a thunderin' sight
O' fun in 't when ye come to light."

MORAL.

I just have room for the moral here:
And this is the moral,—Stick to your sphere.
Or if you insist, as you have the right,
On spreading your wings for a loftier flight,
The moral is,—Take care how you light.

HENRY VAN DYKE
(1852–1933)

NOW ALMOST FORGOTTEN, the Reverend Van Dyke was one of the most widely read American authors of the century's first three decades. His some fifty books include novels, short stories, essays, travel sketches, sermons, literary criticism (he edited a six-volume *Little Masterpieces of English Poetry*) and verse. Born in Germantown, Pennsylvania and later ordained a Presbyterian minister, for many years he pastored the Brick Presbyterian Church in New York City. For twenty-three years he taught English literature at Princeton, his alma mater.

Van Dyke is best known today for his Christmas novella *The Story of the Other Wise Man* (1896). He was so opposed to Germany during the First World War

that he resigned as United States diplomatic minister to the Netherlands (1913–1917) to protest that nation's neutrality.

"America for Me," under the title of "An American in Europe," made its first book appearance in Van Dyke's *The White Bees and Other Poems* (1909). C. Austin Miles set it to music, which was published by Hall-Mack, Philadelphia.

The sixth edition of *Granger's Index to Poetry* (1973) lists seventy-two poems by Van Dyke. Judging from the number of anthologies in which it appeared, "America for Me" has been the most popular. Among his many religious poems, I have selected, "If All the Skies," Van Dyke's effort to explain the mystery of evil, because it turns up in so many collections of Christian verse.

America for Me

'Tis fine to see the Old World, and travel up and down
Among the famous palaces and cities of renown,
To admire the crumbly castles and the statues of the kings,—
But now I think I've had enough of antiquated things.

So it's home again, and home again, America for me!
My heart is turning home again, and there I long to be,
In the land of youth and freedom beyond the ocean bars,
Where the air is full of sunlight and the flag is full of stars.

Oh, London is a man's town, there's power in the air;
And Paris is a woman's town, with flowers in her hair;
And it's sweet to dream in Venice, and it's great to study Rome;
But when it comes to living there is no place like home.

I like the German fir-woods, in green battalions drilled;
I like the gardens of Versailles with flashing fountains filled;
But, oh, to take your hand, my dear, and ramble for a day
In the friendly western woodland where Nature has her way!

I know that Europe's wonderful, yet something seems to lack:
The Past is too much with her, and the people looking back.
But the glory of the Present is to make the Future free,—
We love our land for what she is and what she is to be.

Oh, it's home again, and home again, America for me!
I want a ship that's westward bound to plough the rolling sea,
To the blessed Land of Room Enough beyond the ocean bars,
Where the air is full of sunlight and the flag is full of stars.

If All the Skies

If all the skies were sunshine,
 Our faces would be fain
To feel once more upon them
 The cooling plash of rain.

If all the world were music,
 Our hearts would often long
For one sweet strain of silence,
 To break the endless song.

If life were always merry,
 Our souls would seek relief,
And rest from weary laughter
 In the quiet arms of grief.

WILLIAM ROSS WALLACE
(1819–1881)

WALLACE WAS A Kentucky-born attorney who lived in New York City, where he became a good friend of Edgar Allan Poe. His books of verse include *Alban the Pirate* (a long narrative poem, 1848), *Meditations on America and Other Poems* (1851) and *The Liberty Bell* (1862). The latter contains patriotic poems defending the Union, many of which were set to music.
 Wallace is remembered today only for the last two lines of each stanza in the following poem, originally titled "What Rules the World."

The Hand That Rocks the Cradle

Blessings on the hand of woman!
 Angels guard its strength and grace,
In the palace, cottage, hovel—
 Oh, no matter where the place!
Would that never storms assailed it,
 Rainbows ever round it curled,
For the hand that rocks the cradle
 Is the hand that rocks the world.

Infancy's the tender fountain;
 Power may with beauty flow;

Mother's first to guide the streamlets;
 From them souls unresting grow—
Grow on for the good or evil,
 Sunshine streamed or darkness hurled,
For the hand that rocks the cradle
 Is the hand that rocks the world.

Woman, how divine your mission
 Here upon our natal sod!
Keep, oh keep the young heart open
 Always to the breath of God!
All true trophies of the ages
 Are from mother-love impearled,
For the hand that rocks the cradle
 Is the hand that rocks the world.

Blessings on the hand of woman!
 Fathers, sons and daughters cry;
And the sacred song is mingled
 With the worship in the sky—
Mingles where no tempest darkens,
 Rainbows evermore are hurled,
For the hand that rocks the cradle
 Is the hand that rocks the world.

JOHN WHITAKER WATSON
(1824–1890)

HUNDREDS OF sentimental poems have been written about the tragic deaths of prostitutes—Thomas Hood's "Bridge of Sighs" was England's outstanding example—but no poem on this theme by an American was more recited by "speakers," or more reproduced in nineteenth-century anthologies, than "Beautiful Snow."

The poem was first published in *Harper's Weekly,* November 27, 1858, without a byline. Like so many other anonymous poems that become instant hits, a vigorous controversy arose over who wrote it. As Burton Stevenson relates in *Famous Single Poems,* no less than seven different persons falsely claimed to be its author. "Probably no other poem in American literature," Stevenson comments, "has been so fought over."

There is not the slightest doubt that John Watson wrote the poem, though it was not until his book *Beautiful Snow and Other Poems* appeared in 1869 that his name was officially joined to the poem. The book was first published in 1869 by Turner Brothers, in Philadelphia. An enlarged second edition (1871), printed

by T. B. Peterson, another Philadelphia firm, featured illustrations by Edward L. Henry. More than twenty-five rave reviews were quoted in an appendix to later editions.

A graduate of Columbia University, Watson studied medicine for a time, then abandoned it to become a New York City writer of pathetic verse and romantic fiction for the city's periodicals. He could never understand why only his snow poem became so famous when he had written others that he considered "as good or better." Having read all the poems in his book, I agree with Stevenson that they are a "dreary waste." Next to "Beautiful Snow," his most admired poems were "The Dying Soldier" and "The Patter of Little Feet."

I own a copy of an undated London collection titled *The Thousand Best Poems in the World*, selected by E. W. Cole. "Beautiful Snow" is there credited to Major William Andrew H. Sigourney, who published it as his own in *Galaxy Magazine* (July 1869). Here is how the poem's origin is described:

> In 1850, W. A. Sigourney, a nephew of the late Mrs. L. H. Sigourney, married a wealthy and accomplished young lady in New York City. They soon after went to Europe, where they remained two years, and where she yielded to the tempter and lost her purity and fidelity. On her return home her parents discarded her, and, being shunned and disgraced, she plunged headlong into vice and dissipation. Her husband, as charitable and kind as he was devoted, tried every means to reclaim her to duty, without avail. She sank deeper and deeper in vice, until she was arrested as a common outcast, and sent to the work-house. Being liberated by a well known magistrate, she promised to reform, and for a short time lived with her husband; but in the autumn of 1853 she returned to her old haunts, began to drink to excess, and thus continued until one stormy night of December, when she died in White Street, and was found in the morning nearly covered with snow. She was buried by her husband in Greenwood.

Sigourney's version plagiarizes all the stanzas of Watson's original, adding six absurd new stanzas to the beginning, one in the middle and two more at the end. For years Sigourney earned a dishonest living by reciting the poem at country fairs.

Sigourney was "the most wonderful of all these claimants," Watson told the *New York World* in 1884, "and the one who gave me the most serious annoyance." The conflict between the two men was discussed in *The Phrenological Journal* (Vol. 50, June 1870, pages 429–30) by an editor who did not take sides. Poems by Sigourney had been published previously in this magazine. The editor wrote that the controversy had been revived by a newspaper report that Sigourney had shot himself and was buried in Greenwood. According to Watson, this was a false story written by Sigourney himself to avoid "arrest for some rascality."

Merle Johnson, in *You Know These Lines!*, quotes from a slip that was tipped into the first edition of *Beautiful Snow and Other Poems*:

> Watson and several of his friends were sitting around the table of a Broadway saloon one snowy day, when a poor, half-clad woman

entered and, approaching the party, asked for assistance, at the same time remarking, "Gentlemen, there is nothing *pure* about me except the snow." Watson immediately conceived the idea of the beautiful and touching production which has appealed to thousands of hearts.

I am told that many responses were written to Watson's poem. Included here is one I found in *The Speaker's Garland* 1, no. 2 (1872), Choice Selections. All I could learn about the author, Sallie J. Hancock, was that she was a Kentucky poet and novelist, with one book of verse titled *Rayon d'Amour* (1869).

So many parodies of "Beautiful Snow" were written that an anonymous writer wrote a parody about the parodies:

> Oh! the snow, the beautiful snow
> (This is a parody, please, you know;
> Over and over again you may meet
> Parodies writ on this poem so sweet;
> Rhyming, chiming, skipping along,
> Comical bards think they do nothing wrong;
> Striving to follow what others have done,
> One to the number may keep up the fun).
> Beautiful snow, so gently you scud,
> Pure for a minute, then dirty as mud!
>
> Oh, the snow, the beautiful snow!
> Here 's a fine mess you have left us below;
> Chilling our feet to the tips of our toes;
> Cheekily landing full pert on our nose;
> Jinking, slinking, ever you try
> 'Neath our umbrella to flop in our eye;
> Gamins await us at every new street,
> Watching us carefully, guiding our feet,
> Joking, mocking, ready to throw
> A hard-compressed ball of this beautiful snow.

When Watson's poem was first published it had a final stanza which he wisely omitted from its book version:

> Helpless and frail as the trampled-on snow,
> Sinner, despair not—Christ stoopeth low
> To rescue the soul that is lost in its sin,
> And raise it to life and enjoyment again.
> Groaning,
> Bleeding,
> Dying for thee,
> The Crucified hung on the accursed tree.
> His accents of mercy fall soft on my ear;
> Is there mercy for me, will he heed my weak prayer?
> O God, in the stream that for sinners doth flow,
> Wash me, and I shall be whiter than snow.

Beautiful Snow

Oh! the snow, the beautiful snow,
Filling the sky and the earth below;
Over the house-tops, over the street,
Over the heads of the people you meet;
 Dancing,
 Flirting,
 Skimming along.
Beautiful snow! it can do nothing wrong.
Flying to kiss a fair lady's cheek;
Clinging to lips in a frolicsome freak.
Beautiful snow, from the heavens above,
Pure as an angel and fickle as love!

Oh! the snow, the beautiful snow!
How the flakes gather and laugh as they go!
Whirling about in its maddening fun,
It plays in its glee with every one.
 Chasing,
 Laughing,
 Hurrying by,
It lights up the face and it sparkles the eye;
And even the dogs, with a bark and a bound,
Snap at the crystals that eddy around.
The town is alive, and its heart in a glow
To welcome the coming of beautiful snow.

How the wild crowd goes swaying along,
Hailing each other with humor and song!
How the gay sledges like meteors flash by—
Bright for a moment, then lost to the eye.
 Ringing,
 Swinging,
 Dashing they go
Over the crest of the beautiful snow:
Snow so pure when it falls from the sky,
To be trampled in mud by the crowd rushing by;
To be trampled and tracked by the thousands of feet
Till it blends with the horrible filth in the street.

Once I was pure as the snow—but I fell:
Fell, like the snow-flakes, from heaven—to hell:
Fell, to be tramped as the filth of the street:

Fell, to be scoffed, to be spit on and beat.
 Pleading,
 Cursing,
 Dreading to die,
Selling my soul to whoever would buy,
Dealing in shame for a morsel of bread,
Hating the living and fearing the dead.
Merciful God! have I fallen so low?
And yet I was once like this beautiful snow!

Once I was fair as the beautiful snow,
With an eye like its crystals, a heart like its glow;
Once I was loved for my innocent grace—
Flattered and sought for the charm of my face.
 Father,
 Mother,
 Sisters all,
God, and myself, I have lost by my fall.
The veriest wretch that goes shivering by
Will take a wide sweep, lest I wander too nigh;
For of all that is on or about me, I know
There is nothing that's pure but the beautiful snow.

How strange it should be that this beautiful snow
Should fall on a sinner with nowhere to go!
How strange it would be, when the night comes again,
If the snow and the ice struck my desperate brain!
 Fainting,
 Freezing,
 Dying alone
Too wicked for prayer, too weak for my moan
To be heard in the crash of the crazy town,
Gone mad in its joy at the snow's coming down
To lie and to die in my terrible woe,
With a bed and a shroud of the beautiful snow.

A Response to "Beautiful Snow"
(by Sallie J. Hancock)

Cast by the bright wings of a seraph—the snow,
From the uppermost heights to the earth below;
Gently enwrapping a star-begemmed spread

O'er homes of the living and graves of the dead.
Radiantly white as the Genii of story!
Pure as the saints in their robings of glory!
Whose soft tears of sympathy froze in their fall,
For the sin and the curse that are over us all;
Fleecy and light from the olive-hued skies,
As the trailing insignia of paradise;
The one fair perishing thing that is given
To worlds aglow with the splendors of Heaven!

Proud spirit, who told of the height which you fell
Adown "like the snow flakes from Heaven to hell?"
God made you as fair as the beautiful snow!
He loves you, poor sinner, though you may not know
How deep in that Infinite heart sank your cry
For "shelter" and "rest" of the *saint* passing by,
Who spurned you, and left you to die in the street,
With a bed and a shroud of the snow and the sleet.
The world has cursed you, yet *God has not said*
A soul shall be bartered for gold or for bread.

He knows all your erring and horrible woe,
The want and the crime that have maddened you so:
All the dearer to him for the strife, and for stain,
And *purer* to-day for repentance and pain!
Made white by His blood, as the beautiful snow
"That falls on a sinner with nowhere to go;"
And sweeter the pardon hard won by the cries
That from Magdalen lips went up to the skies.

Oh! beautiful snow, from the filth of the earth,
Swift rises again in its cherubic mirth
In crystalline dew-drops—all glistening bright
As clear shining stars in a heaven of night.
If contrite to the throne of God's mercy you go,
He will make you as pure as the "beautiful snow!"

EDWARD JEWITT WHEELER
(1859–1922)

BORN IN CLEVELAND, Wheeler settled in New York City where he edited several
periodicals including the *Literary Digest*, and served a term as president of the
Poetry Society of America. He authored several nonfiction books, and at least

one volume of poetry, *Stories in Rhyme for Holiday Time* (1894). The two poems chosen here are the only two I found anthologized, one light-hearted, the other a serious, well-crafted sonnet.

"Alleys" are superior marbles, and "commons" are common marbles. I had no notion of what "phen-dubs" meant until William Harmon, a professor of English at the University of North Carolina, Chapel Hill, had the impulse to check a variant spelling, "fen-dubs," in the *Dictionary of American Regional English*. It, too, is a term used in marble games. If a player knocks two marbles out of the ring in one shot, he can say "dubs" and keep both marbles. But if his opponent shouts "fen-dubs" it prohibits the shooter from altering the rules, and he must put one marble back. "Fen" is a corruption of fend, meaning to forbid, and "dubs" refers to doubling.

"Onery twoery ickery ann" was an old counting-out rhyme like "Eenie, meenie, miney, mo" and "Ibbity, bibbity, sibbity, sab." The exact words varied widely. For the full jingle, see *Rainbow in the Sky* (1935), an anthology edited by Louis Untermeyer.

The Boy to the Schoolmaster

You've quizzed me often and puzzled me long,
 You've asked me to cipher and spell,
You've called me a dunce if I answered wrong,
 Or a dolt if I failed to tell
Just when to say *lie* and when to say *lay*,
 Or what nine sevens may make,
Or the longitude of Kamschatka Bay,
 Or the I-forget-what's-its-name Lake,
So I think its about *my* turn, I do,
 To ask a question or so of you.

The schoolmaster grim, he opened his eyes,
But said not a word for sheer surprise.

Can you tell what "phen-dubs" means? I can.
 Can you say all off by heart
The "onery twoery ickery ann,"
 Or tell "alleys" and "commons" apart?
Can *you* fling a top, I would like to know,
 Till it hums like a bumble-bee?
Can you make a kite yourself that will go
 'Most as high as the eye can see,
Till it sails and soars like a hawk on the wing,
And the little birds come and light on its string?

The schoolmaster looked oh! very demure,
But his mouth was twitching, I'm almost sure.

Can you tell where the nest of the oriole swings,
 Or the color its eggs may be?
Do you know the time when the squirrel brings
 Its young from their nest in the tree?
Can you tell when the chestnuts are ready to drop
 Or where the best hazel-nuts grow?
Can you climb a high tree to the very tip-top,
 Then gaze without trembling below?
Can you swim and dive, can you jump and run,
Or do anything else we boys call fun?

The master's voice trembled as he replied:
"You are right, my lad, I'm the dunce," he sighed.

Night's Mardi Gras

Night is the true democracy. When day
 Like some great monarch with his train has passed,
 In regal pomp and splendor to the last,
The stars troop forth along the Milky Way,
A jostling crowd, in radiant disarray,
 On heaven's broad boulevard in pageants vast.
 And things of earth, the hunted and outcast,
Come from their haunts and hiding-places; yea,
Even from the nooks and crannies of the mind
 Visions uncouth and vagrant fancies start,
 And specters of dead joy, that shun the light,
And impotent regrets and terrors blind,
 Each one, in form grotesque, playing its part
 In the fantastic Mardi Gras of Night.

JOHN GREENLEAF WHITTIER
(1807–1892)

WHITTIER'S TWO best known poems, "The Barefoot Boy" and "Maud Muller,"
with a brief sketch of his life, are in this book's "prequel," *Best Remembered
Poems*. Here I reprint in full (most anthologies contain only a portion) "The

Eternal Goodness," his most admired religious poem. Nothing he wrote so eloquently expressed his simple Quaker faith, and his abhorrence of Calvinism's belief in eternal punishment for the unsaved—a doctrine that made God eternally evil. It was first printed in *The Independent* (March 16, 1865) and later in *The Tent on the Beach and Other Poems* (1867).

"Barbara Frietchie" is seldom in today's schoolbooks, partly because of its historical inaccuracy. The first person to display the Union flag in 1862, when Stonewall Jackson marched his men through Frederick, Maryland, was a young woman. Not until northern troops entered the town a week later did Barbara do the same. It doesn't matter, because Whittier's poem can still be enjoyed, and " 'Shoot, if you must, this old grey head' " is a line not easily forgotten.

"Barbara Frietchie" first appeared in the *Atlantic Monthly* (October 1863), without a byline, and later in Whittier's *In War Time and Other Poems* (1864). He based the story on a letter from Mrs. Southworth, a writer of some sixty sensational romantic novels, all now forgotten but then avidly devoured by women. She had the unusual maiden name of Emma Dorothy Eliza Novitte, the initials of which spell EDEN. Whittier thanked her with a handwritten copy of his poem and a note saying, "If it is good for anything, thee deserves all the credit."

The Eternal Goodness

O Friends! with whom my feet have trod
 The quiet aisles of prayer,
Glad witness to your zeal for God
 And love of man I bear.

I trace your lines of argument;
 Your logic linked and strong
I weigh as one who dreads dissent,
 And fears a doubt as wrong.

But still my human hands are weak
 To hold your iron creeds:
Against the words ye bid me speak
 My heart within me pleads.

Who fathoms the Eternal Thought?
 Who talks of scheme and plan?
The Lord is God! He needeth not
 The poor device of man.

I walk with bare, hushed feet the ground
 Ye tread with boldness shod;

I dare not fix with mete and bound
 The love and power of God.

Ye praise His justice; even such
 His pitying love I deem:
Ye seek a king; I fain would touch
 The robe that hath no seam.

Ye see the curse which overbroods
 A world of pain and loss;
I hear our Lord's beatitudes
 And prayer upon the cross.

More than your schoolmen teach, within
 Myself, alas! I know:
Too dark ye cannot paint the sin,
 Too small the merit show.

I bow my forehead to the dust,
 I veil mine eyes for shame,
And urge, in trembling self-distrust,
 A prayer without a claim.

I see the wrong that round me lies,
 I feel the guilt within;
I hear, with groan and travail-cries,
 The world confess its sin.

Yet, in the maddening maze of things,
 And tossed by storm and flood,
To one fixed trust my spirit clings;
 I know that God is good!

Not mine to look where cherubim
 And seraphs may not see,
But nothing can be good in Him
 Which evil is in me.

The wrong that pains my soul below
 I dare not throne above;
I know not of His hate,—I know
 His goodness and His love.

I dimly guess from blessings known
 Of greater out of sight,
And, with the chastened Psalmist, own
 His judgments too are right.

I long for household voices gone,
 For vanished smiles I long,
But God hath led my dear ones on,
 And He can do no wrong.

I know not what the future hath
 Of marvel or surprise,
Assured alone that life and death
 His mercy underlies.

And if my heart and flesh are weak
 To bear an untried pain,
The bruised reed He will not break,
 But strengthen and sustain.

No offering of my own I have,
 Nor works my faith to prove;
I can but give the gifts He gave,
 And plead His love for love.

And so beside the Silent Sea
 I wait the muffled oar;
No harm from Him can come to me
 On ocean or on shore.

I know not where His islands lift
 Their fronded palms in air;
I only know I cannot drift
 Beyond His love and care.

O brothers! if my faith is vain,
 If hopes like these betray,
Pray for me that my feet may gain
 The sure and safer way.

And Thou, O Lord! by whom are seen
 Thy creatures as they be,
Forgive me if too close I lean
 My human heart on Thee!

Barbara Frietchie

Up from the meadows rich with corn,
Clear in the cool September morn,

The clustered spires of Frederick stand
Green-walled by the hills of Maryland.

Round and about them orchards sweep,
Apple and peach tree fruited deep,

Fair as a garden of the Lord
To the eyes of the famished rebel horde;

On that pleasant morn of the early fall
When Lee marched over the mountain wall,

Over the mountains winding down,
Horse and foot into Frederick town.

Forty flags with their silver stars,
Forty flags with their crimson bars,

Flapped in the morning wind: the sun
Of noon looked down, and saw not one.

Up rose old Barbara Frietchie then,
Bowed with her fourscore years and ten;

Bravest of all in Frederick town,
She took up the flag the men hauled down;

In her attic window the staff she set,
To show that one heart was loyal yet.

Up the street came the rebel tread,
Stonewall Jackson riding ahead.

Under his slouched hat left and right
He glanced; the old flag met his sight.

"Halt!"—the dust-brown ranks stood fast.
"Fire!"—out blazed the rifle-blast.

It shivered the window, pane and sash;
It rent the banner with seam and gash.

Quick, as it fell, from the broken staff
Dame Barbara snatched the silken scarf;

She leaned far out on the window-sill,
And shook it forth with a royal will.

"Shoot, if you must, this old grey head,
But spare your country's flag!" she said.

A shade of sadness, a blush of shame,
Over the face of the leader came;

The nobler nature within him stirred
To life at that woman's deed and word:

"Who touches a hair of yon grey head
Dies like a dog! March on!" he said.

All day long through Frederick street
Sounded the tread of marching feet:

All day long that free flag tost
Over the heads of the rebel host.

Ever its torn folds rose and fell
On the loyal winds that loved it well;

And through the hill-gaps sunset light
Shone over it with a warm good-night.

REVEREND CHARLES WOLFE
(1791–1823)

WOLFE'S ELEGY ON the death of Sir John Moore, one of England's best-loved poems, became almost as much admired in the United States. Moore was a renowned British general who died in 1809 in the Peninsular War while leading his troops in Corunna, Spain, to a victorious battle against Napoleon's army. The general was carried off the field, mortally wounded, and buried before dawn.

Charles Wolfe, a Church of England curate born in Dublin, was said to have based his elegy on an account of Moore's death by Robert Southey. The poem appeared in the *Newry Telegraph* in 1817. A book of Wolfe's poems was posthumously published in 1903, but only this one has survived in hundreds of anthologies.

A few scribblers falsely claimed authorship of the elegy, and there have been many parodies. At least two of the best took "burial" as a euphemism for "married." Phoebe Cary—she and her sister Alice were both popular nineteenth-century versifiers—wrote "The Marriage of Sir John Smith," which begins:

> Not a sigh was heard, nor a funeral tone,
> As the man to his bridal we hurried;
> Not a woman discharged her farewell groan,
> On the spot where the fellow was married.

An anonymous parodist opened "The Burial of the Bachelor" this way:

> Not a laugh was heard, not a frivolous note,
> As the groom to the wedding we carried;
> Not a jester discharged his farewell shot
> As the bachelor went to be married.

Sir Robert Ball, the Irish Astronomer Royal, found an historical error in the second stanza of Wolfe's poem. It seems there could not have been any misty light from the moon because it had long set before the burial took place.

So well known was the poem, observed William Harmon, that Thoreau quoted its first stanza, in his famous essay on civil disobedience, without identifying the poem or its author.

The Burial of Sir John Moore

Not a drum was heard, not a funeral note,
 As his corse to the ramparts we hurried;
Not a soldier discharged his farewell shot
 O'er the grave where our hero we buried.

We buried him darkly, at dead of night,
 The sods with our bayonets turning,
By the struggling moonbeam's misty light,
 And the lantern dimly burning.

No useless coffin enclosed his breast,
 Not in sheet nor in shroud we wound him;
But he lay like a warrior taking his rest,
 With his martial cloak around him.

Few and short were the prayers we said,
 And we spoke not a word of sorrow;
But we steadfastly gazed on the face that was dead,
 And we bitterly thought of the morrow.

We thought as we hollow'd his narrow bed,
 And smoothed down his lonely pillow,
That the foe and the stranger would tread o'er his head,
 And we far away on the billow!

Lightly they'll talk of the spirit that's gone,
 And o'er his cold ashes upbraid him;

But little he'll reck if they let him sleep on,
 In the grave where a Briton has laid him.

But half of our heavy task was done,
 When the clock struck the hour for retiring,
And we heard the distant and random gun
 That the foe was sullenly firing.

Slowly and sadly we laid him down,
 From the field of his fame fresh and gory;
We carved not a line, and we raised not a stone,
 But we left him alone in his glory.

HENRY CLAY WORK
(1832–1884)

"GRANDFATHER'S CLOCK" may be a bit out of place here because it is a song whose words and music were both written by Work. I include it because its lyrics appeared in so many pre-1900 collections of popular verse.

Work was born in Middletown, Connecticut, and raised in Quincy, Illinois. When his family moved back to Middletown, young Work learned the printing trade and taught himself music. He worked in Chicago as a printer from 1854 until his numerous Union songs of the Civil War brought him fame. They include "Grafted into the Army," "Kingdom Coming," "Babylon Is Fallen" and "Marching through Georgia," a song celebrating Major General William Sherman's famous march to Savannah. Among his temperance songs, the most frequently sung was about a drunk that begins, "Father, dear father, come home with me now." It, too, turns up in many nineteenth-century verse anthologies.

"Grandfather's Clock," Work's most successful non-war song, was published in 1876 and first sung in a minstrel show. His nephew, Bertram G. Work, gathered his uncle's songs into a book titled *The Songs of Henry Clay Work* (c. 1885), which had many later editions.

Grandfather's Clock

My grandfather's clock was too large for the shelf,
 So it stood ninety years on the floor;
It was taller by half than the old man himself,
 Though it weighed not a pennyweight more.
It was bought on the morn of the day that he was born
 And was always his treasure and pride.
But it stopped short—never to go again—
 When the old man died.

Ninety years without slumbering
 Tick, tick, tick, tick.
His life-seconds numbering
 Tick, tick, tick, tick.
It stopped short—never to go again—
 When the old man died.

In watching its pendulum swing to and fro
 Many hours had he spent while a boy;
And in childhood and manhood the clock seemed to know
 And to share both his grief and his joy,
For it struck twenty-four when he entered the door
 With a blooming and beautiful bride,
But it stopped short—never to go again—
 When the old man died.

My grandfather said of those he could hire,
 Not a servant so faithful he found,
For it wasted no time and had but one desire—
 At the close of each week to be wound.
And it kept in its place—not a frown upon its face,
 And its hands never hung by its side;
But it stopped short—never to go again—
 When the old man died.

It rang an alarm in the dead of night—
 An alarm that for years had been dumb.
And we knew that his spirit was pluming for flight
 That his hour for departure had come.
Still the clock kept the time with a soft and muffled chime
 As we silently stood by his side;
But it stopped short—never to go again—
 When the old man died.

ALPHABETICAL LIST OF TITLES

ALPHABETICAL LIST OF FIRST LINES

A CATALOG OF SELECTED
DOVER BOOKS
IN ALL FIELDS OF INTEREST

A CATALOG OF SELECTED DOVER
BOOKS IN ALL FIELDS OF INTEREST

CONCERNING THE SPIRITUAL IN ART, Wassily Kandinsky. Pioneering work by father of abstract art. Thoughts on color theory, nature of art. Analysis of earlier masters. 12 illustrations. 80pp. of text. 5⅜ × 8½. 23411-8 Pa. $3.95

ANIMALS: 1,419 Copyright-Free Illustrations of Mammals, Birds, Fish, Insects, etc., Jim Harter (ed.). Clear wood engravings present, in extremely lifelike poses, over 1,000 species of animals. One of the most extensive pictorial sourcebooks of its kind. Captions. Index. 284pp. 9 × 12. 23766-4 Pa. $11.95

CELTIC ART: The Methods of Construction, George Bain. Simple geometric techniques for making Celtic interlacements, spirals, Kells-type initials, animals, humans, etc. Over 500 illustrations. 160pp. 9 × 12. (USO) 22923-8 Pa. $8.95

AN ATLAS OF ANATOMY FOR ARTISTS, Fritz Schider. Most thorough reference work on art anatomy in the world. Hundreds of illustrations, including selections from works by Vesalius, Leonardo, Goya, Ingres, Michelangelo, others. 593 illustrations. 192pp. 7⅛ × 10¼. 20241-0 Pa. $8.95

CELTIC HAND STROKE-BY-STROKE (Irish Half-Uncial from "The Book of Kells"): An Arthur Baker Calligraphy Manual, Arthur Baker. Complete guide to creating each letter of the alphabet in distinctive Celtic manner. Covers hand position, strokes, pens, inks, paper, more. Illustrated. 48pp. 8¼ × 11.
 24336-2 Pa. $3.95

EASY ORIGAMI, John Montroll. Charming collection of 32 projects (hat, cup, pelican, piano, swan, many more) specially designed for the novice origami hobbyist. Clearly illustrated easy-to-follow instructions insure that even beginning papercrafters will achieve successful results. 48pp. 8¼ × 11. 27298-2 Pa. $2.95

THE COMPLETE BOOK OF BIRDHOUSE CONSTRUCTION FOR WOOD-WORKERS, Scott D. Campbell. Detailed instructions, illustrations, tables. Also data on bird habitat and instinct patterns. Bibliography. 3 tables. 63 illustrations in 15 figures. 48pp. 5¼ × 8½. 24407-5 Pa. $1.95

BLOOMINGDALE'S ILLUSTRATED 1886 CATALOG: Fashions, Dry Goods and Housewares, Bloomingdale Brothers. Famed merchants' extremely rare catalog depicting about 1,700 products: clothing, housewares, firearms, dry goods, jewelry, more. Invaluable for dating, identifying vintage items. Also, copyright-free graphics for artists, designers. Co-published with Henry Ford Museum & Greenfield Village. 160pp. 8¼ × 11. 25780-0 Pa. $9.95

HISTORIC COSTUME IN PICTURES, Braun & Schneider. Over 1,450 costumed figures in clearly detailed engravings—from dawn of civilization to end of 19th century. Captions. Many folk costumes. 256pp. 8⅜ × 11¼. 23150-X Pa. $10.95

STICKLEY CRAFTSMAN FURNITURE CATALOGS, Gustav Stickley and L. & J. G. Stickley. Beautiful, functional furniture in two authentic catalogs from 1910. 594 illustrations, including 277 photos, show settles, rockers, armchairs, reclining chairs, bookcases, desks, tables. 183pp. 6½ × 9¼. 23838-5 Pa. $8.95

AMERICAN LOCOMOTIVES IN HISTORIC PHOTOGRAPHS: 1858 to 1949, Ron Ziel (ed.). A rare collection of 126 meticulously detailed official photographs, called "builder portraits," of American locomotives that majestically chronicle the rise of steam locomotive power in America. Introduction. Detailed captions. xi + 129pp. 9 × 12. 27393-8 Pa. $12.95

AMERICA'S LIGHTHOUSES: An Illustrated History, Francis Ross Holland, Jr. Delightfully written, profusely illustrated fact-filled survey of over 200 American lighthouses since 1716. History, anecdotes, technological advances, more. 240pp. 8 × 10¾. 25576-X Pa. $11.95

TOWARDS A NEW ARCHITECTURE, Le Corbusier. Pioneering manifesto by founder of "International School." Technical and aesthetic theories, views of industry, economics, relation of form to function, "mass-production split" and much more. Profusely illustrated. 320pp. 6⅛ × 9¼. (USO) 25023-7 Pa. $8.95

HOW THE OTHER HALF LIVES, Jacob Riis. Famous journalistic record, exposing poverty and degradation of New York slums around 1900, by major social reformer. 100 striking and influential photographs. 233pp. 10 × 7⅞.
22012-5 Pa $10.95

FRUIT KEY AND TWIG KEY TO TREES AND SHRUBS, William M. Harlow. One of the handiest and most widely used identification aids. Fruit key covers 120 deciduous and evergreen species; twig key 160 deciduous species. Easily used. Over 300 photographs. 126pp. 5⅜ × 8½. 20511-8 Pa. $3.95

COMMON BIRD SONGS, Dr. Donald J. Borror. Songs of 60 most common U.S. birds: robins, sparrows, cardinals, bluejays, finches, more—arranged in order of increasing complexity. Up to 9 variations of songs of each species.
Cassette and manual 99911-4 $8.95

ORCHIDS AS HOUSE PLANTS, Rebecca Tyson Northen. Grow cattleyas and many other kinds of orchids—in a window, in a case, or under artificial light. 63 illustrations. 148pp. 5⅜ × 8½. 23261-1 Pa. $3.95

MONSTER MAZES, Dave Phillips. Masterful mazes at four levels of difficulty. Avoid deadly perils and evil creatures to find magical treasures. Solutions for all 32 exciting illustrated puzzles. 48pp. 8¼ × 11. 26005-4 Pa. $2.95

MOZART'S DON GIOVANNI (DOVER OPERA LIBRETTO SERIES), Wolfgang Amadeus Mozart. Introduced and translated by Ellen H. Bleiler. Standard Italian libretto, with complete English translation. Convenient and thoroughly portable—an ideal companion for reading along with a recording or the performance itself. Introduction. List of characters. Plot summary. 121pp. 5¼ × 8½.
24944-1 Pa. $2.95

TECHNICAL MANUAL AND DICTIONARY OF CLASSICAL BALLET, Gail Grant. Defines, explains, comments on steps, movements, poses and concepts. 15-page pictorial section. Basic book for student, viewer. 127pp. 5⅜ × 8½.
21843-0 Pa. $3.95

BRASS INSTRUMENTS: Their History and Development, Anthony Baines. Authoritative, updated survey of the evolution of trumpets, trombones, bugles, cornets, French horns, tubas and other brass wind instruments. Over 140 illustrations and 48 music examples. Corrected and updated by author. New preface. Bibliography. 320pp. 5⅜ × 8½. 27574-4 Pa. $9.95

HOLLYWOOD GLAMOR PORTRAITS, John Kobal (ed.). 145 photos from 1926–49. Harlow, Gable, Bogart, Bacall; 94 stars in all. Full background on photographers, technical aspects. 160pp. 8⅜ × 11¼. 23352-9 Pa. $9.95

MAX AND MORITZ, Wilhelm Busch. Great humor classic in both German and English. Also 10 other works: "Cat and Mouse," "Plisch and Plumm," etc. 216pp. 5⅜ × 8½. 20181-3 Pa. $5.95

THE RAVEN AND OTHER FAVORITE POEMS, Edgar Allan Poe. Over 40 of the author's most memorable poems: "The Bells," "Ulalume," "Israfel," "To Helen," "The Conqueror Worm," "Eldorado," "Annabel Lee," many more. Alphabetic lists of titles and first lines. 64pp. 5³⁄₁₆ × 8¼. 26685-0 Pa. $1.00

SEVEN SCIENCE FICTION NOVELS, H. G. Wells. The standard collection of the great novels. Complete, unabridged. First Men in the Moon, Island of Dr. Moreau, War of the Worlds, Food of the Gods, Invisible Man, Time Machine, In the Days of the Comet. Total of 1,015pp. 5⅜ × 8½. (USO) 20264-X Clothbd. $29.95

AMULETS AND SUPERSTITIONS, E. A. Wallis Budge. Comprehensive discourse on origin, powers of amulets in many ancient cultures: Arab, Persian, Babylonian, Assyrian, Egyptian, Gnostic, Hebrew, Phoenician, Syriac, etc. Covers cross, swastika, crucifix, seals, rings, stones, etc. 584pp. 5⅜ × 8½. 23573-4 Pa. $12.95

RUSSIAN STORIES/PYCCKNE PACCKA3bl: A Dual-Language Book, edited by Gleb Struve. Twelve tales by such masters as Chekhov, Tolstoy, Dostoevsky, Pushkin, others. Excellent word-for-word English translations on facing pages, plus teaching and study aids, Russian/English vocabulary, biographical/critical introductions, more. 416pp. 5⅜ × 8½. 26244-8 Pa. $8.95

PHILADELPHIA THEN AND NOW: 60 Sites Photographed in the Past and Present, Kenneth Finkel and Susan Oyama. Rare photographs of City Hall, Logan Square, Independence Hall, Betsy Ross House, other landmarks juxtaposed with contemporary views. Captures changing face of historic city. Introduction. Captions. 128pp. 8¼ × 11. 25790-8 Pa. $9.95

AIA ARCHITECTURAL GUIDE TO NASSAU AND SUFFOLK COUNTIES, LONG ISLAND, The American Institute of Architects, Long Island Chapter, and the Society for the Preservation of Long Island Antiquities. Comprehensive, well-researched and generously illustrated volume brings to life over three centuries of Long Island's great architectural heritage. More than 240 photographs with authoritative, extensively detailed captions. 176pp. 8¼ × 11. 26946-9 Pa. $14.95

NORTH AMERICAN INDIAN LIFE: Customs and Traditions of 23 Tribes, Elsie Clews Parsons (ed.). 27 fictionalized essays by noted anthropologists examine religion, customs, government, additional facets of life among the Winnebago, Crow, Zuni, Eskimo, other tribes. 480pp. 6⅛ × 9¼. 27377-6 Pa. $10.95

FRANK LLOYD WRIGHT'S HOLLYHOCK HOUSE, Donald Hoffmann. Lavishly illustrated, carefully documented study of one of Wright's most controversial residential designs. Over 120 photographs, floor plans, elevations, etc. Detailed perceptive text by noted Wright scholar. Index. 128pp. 9¼ × 10¾.
27133-1 Pa. $11.95

THE MALE AND FEMALE FIGURE IN MOTION: 60 Classic Photographic Sequences, Eadweard Muybridge. 60 true-action photographs of men and women walking, running, climbing, bending, turning, etc., reproduced from rare 19th-century masterpiece. vi + 121pp. 9 × 12. 24745-7 Pa. $10.95

1001 QUESTIONS ANSWERED ABOUT THE SEASHORE, N. J. Berrill and Jacquelyn Berrill. Queries answered about dolphins, sea snails, sponges, starfish, fishes, shore birds, many others. Covers appearance, breeding, growth, feeding, much more. 305pp. 5¼ × 8¼. 23366-9 Pa. $7.95

GUIDE TO OWL WATCHING IN NORTH AMERICA, Donald S. Heintzelman. Superb guide offers complete data and descriptions of 19 species: barn owl, screech owl, snowy owl, many more. Expert coverage of owl-watching equipment, conservation, migrations and invasions, etc. Guide to observing sites. 84 illustrations. xiii + 193pp. 5⅜ × 8½. 27344-X Pa. $7.95

MEDICINAL AND OTHER USES OF NORTH AMERICAN PLANTS: A Historical Survey with Special Reference to the Eastern Indian Tribes, Charlotte Erichsen-Brown. Chronological historical citations document 500 years of usage of plants, trees, shrubs native to eastern Canada, northeastern U.S. Also complete identifying information. 343 illustrations. 544pp. 6½ × 9¼. 25951-X Pa. $12.95

STORYBOOK MAZES, Dave Phillips. 23 stories and mazes on two-page spreads: Wizard of Oz, Treasure Island, Robin Hood, etc. Solutions. 64pp. 8¼ × 11.
23628-5 Pa. $2.95

NEGRO FOLK MUSIC, U.S.A., Harold Courlander. Noted folklorist's scholarly yet readable analysis of rich and varied musical tradition. Includes authentic versions of over 40 folk songs. Valuable bibliography and discography. xi + 324pp. 5⅜ × 8½. 27350-4 Pa. $7.95

MOVIE-STAR PORTRAITS OF THE FORTIES, John Kobal (ed.). 163 glamor, studio photos of 106 stars of the 1940s: Rita Hayworth, Ava Gardner, Marlon Brando, Clark Gable, many more. 176pp. 8⅜ × 11¼. 23546-7 Pa. $10.95

BENCHLEY LOST AND FOUND, Robert Benchley. Finest humor from early 30s, about pet peeves, child psychologists, post office and others. Mostly unavailable elsewhere. 73 illustrations by Peter Arno and others. 183pp. 5⅜ × 8½.
22410-4 Pa. $5.95

YEKL and THE IMPORTED BRIDEGROOM AND OTHER STORIES OF YIDDISH NEW YORK, Abraham Cahan. Film Hester Street based on Yekl (1896). Novel, other stories among first about Jewish immigrants on N.Y.'s East Side. 240pp. 5⅜ × 8½. 22427-9 Pa. $5.95

SELECTED POEMS, Walt Whitman. Generous sampling from *Leaves of Grass*. Twenty-four poems include "I Hear America Singing," "Song of the Open Road," "I Sing the Body Electric," "When Lilacs Last in the Dooryard Bloom'd," "O Captain! My Captain!"—all reprinted from an authoritative edition. Lists of titles and first lines. 128pp. 5³⁄₁₆ × 8¼. 26878-0 Pa. $1.00

CATALOG OF DOVER BOOKS

THE BEST TALES OF HOFFMANN, E. T. A. Hoffmann. 10 of Hoffmann's most important stories: "Nutcracker and the King of Mice," "The Golden Flowerpot," etc. 458pp. 5⅜ × 8½. 21793-0 Pa. $8.95

FROM FETISH TO GOD IN ANCIENT EGYPT, E. A. Wallis Budge. Rich detailed survey of Egyptian conception of "God" and gods, magic, cult of animals, Osiris, more. Also, superb English translations of hymns and legends. 240 illustrations. 545pp. 5⅜ × 8½. 25803-3 Pa. $11.95

FRENCH STORIES/CONTES FRANÇAIS: A Dual-Language Book, Wallace Fowlie. Ten stories by French masters, Voltaire to Camus: "Micromegas" by Voltaire; "The Atheist's Mass" by Balzac; "Minuet" by de Maupassant; "The Guest" by Camus, six more. Excellent English translations on facing pages. Also French-English vocabulary list, exercises, more. 352pp. 5⅜ × 8½. 26443-2 Pa. $8.95

CHICAGO AT THE TURN OF THE CENTURY IN PHOTOGRAPHS: 122 Historic Views from the Collections of the Chicago Historical Society, Larry A. Viskochil. Rare large-format prints offer detailed views of City Hall, State Street, the Loop, Hull House, Union Station, many other landmarks, circa 1904–1913. Introduction. Captions. Maps. 144pp. 9⅜ × 12¼. 24656-6 Pa. $12.95

OLD BROOKLYN IN EARLY PHOTOGRAPHS, 1865–1929, William Lee Younger. Luna Park, Gravesend race track, construction of Grand Army Plaza, moving of Hotel Brighton, etc. 157 previously unpublished photographs. 165pp. 8⅜ × 11¼. 23587-4 Pa. $12.95

THE MYTHS OF THE NORTH AMERICAN INDIANS, Lewis Spence. Rich anthology of the myths and legends of the Algonquins, Iroquois, Pawnees and Sioux, prefaced by an extensive historical and ethnological commentary. 36 illustrations. 480pp. 5⅜ × 8½. 25967-6 Pa. $8.95

AN ENCYCLOPEDIA OF BATTLES: Accounts of Over 1,560 Battles from 1479 B.C. to the Present, David Eggenberger. Essential details of every major battle in recorded history from the first battle of Megiddo in 1479 B.C. to Grenada in 1984. List of Battle Maps. New Appendix covering the years 1967–1984. Index. 99 illustrations. 544pp. 6½ × 9¼. 24913-1 Pa. $14.95

SAILING ALONE AROUND THE WORLD, Captain Joshua Slocum. First man to sail around the world, alone, in small boat. One of great feats of seamanship told in delightful manner. 67 illustrations. 294pp. 5⅜ × 8½. 20326-3 Pa. $5.95

ANARCHISM AND OTHER ESSAYS, Emma Goldman. Powerful, penetrating, prophetic essays on direct action, role of minorities, prison reform, puritan hypocrisy, violence, etc. 271pp. 5⅜ × 8½. 22484-8 Pa. $5.95

MYTHS OF THE HINDUS AND BUDDHISTS, Ananda K. Coomaraswamy and Sister Nivedita. Great stories of the epics; deeds of Krishna, Shiva, taken from puranas, Vedas, folk tales; etc. 32 illustrations. 400pp. 5⅜ × 8½. 21759-0 Pa. $9.95

BEYOND PSYCHOLOGY, Otto Rank. Fear of death, desire of immortality, nature of sexuality, social organization, creativity, according to Rankian system. 291pp. 5⅜ × 8½. 20485-5 Pa. $7.95

A THEOLOGICO-POLITICAL TREATISE, Benedict Spinoza. Also contains unfinished Political Treatise. Great classic on religious liberty, theory of government on common consent. R. Elwes translation. Total of 421pp. 5⅜ × 8½. 20249-6 Pa. $7.95

MY BONDAGE AND MY FREEDOM, Frederick Douglass. Born a slave, Douglass became outspoken force in antislavery movement. The best of Douglass' autobiographies. Graphic description of slave life. 464pp. 5⅜ × 8½. 22457-0 Pa. $8.95

FOLLOWING THE EQUATOR: A Journey Around the World, Mark Twain. Fascinating humorous account of 1897 voyage to Hawaii, Australia, India, New Zealand, etc. Ironic, bemused reports on peoples, customs, climate, flora and fauna, politics, much more. 197 illustrations. 720pp. 5⅜ × 8½. 26113-1 Pa. $15.95

THE PEOPLE CALLED SHAKERS, Edward D. Andrews. Definitive study of Shakers: origins, beliefs, practices, dances, social organization, furniture and crafts, etc. 33 illustrations. 351pp. 5⅜ × 8½. 21081-2 Pa. $7.95

THE MYTHS OF GREECE AND ROME, H. A. Guerber. A classic of mythology, generously illustrated, long prized for its simple, graphic, accurate retelling of the principal myths of Greece and Rome, and for its commentary on their origins and significance. With 64 illustrations by Michelangelo, Raphael, Titian, Rubens, Canova, Bernini and others. 480pp. 5⅜ × 8½. 27584-1 Pa. $9.95

PSYCHOLOGY OF MUSIC, Carl E. Seashore. Classic work discusses music as a medium from psychological viewpoint. Clear treatment of physical acoustics, auditory apparatus, sound perception, development of musical skills, nature of musical feeling, host of other topics. 88 figures. 408pp. 5⅜ × 8½. 21851-1 Pa. $9.95

THE PHILOSOPHY OF HISTORY, Georg W. Hegel. Great classic of Western thought develops concept that history is not chance but rational process, the evolution of freedom. 457pp. 5⅜ × 8½. 20112-0 Pa. $8.95

THE BOOK OF TEA, Kakuzo Okakura. Minor classic of the Orient: entertaining, charming explanation, interpretation of traditional Japanese culture in terms of tea ceremony. 94pp. 5⅜ × 8½. 20070-1 Pa. $2.95

LIFE IN ANCIENT EGYPT, Adolf Erman. Fullest, most thorough, detailed older account with much not in more recent books, domestic life, religion, magic, medicine, commerce, much more. Many illustrations reproduce tomb paintings, carvings, hieroglyphs, etc. 597pp. 5⅜ × 8½. 22632-8 Pa. $9.95

SUNDIALS, Their Theory and Construction, Albert Waugh. Far and away the best, most thorough coverage of ideas, mathematics concerned, types, construction, adjusting anywhere. Simple, nontechnical treatment allows even children to build several of these dials. Over 100 illustrations. 230pp. 5⅜ × 8½. 22947-5 Pa. $5.95

DYNAMICS OF FLUIDS IN POROUS MEDIA, Jacob Bear. For advanced students of ground water hydrology, soil mechanics and physics, drainage and irrigation engineering, and more. 335 illustrations. Exercises, with answers. 784pp. 6⅛ × 9¼. 65675-6 Pa. $19.95

SONGS OF EXPERIENCE: Facsimile Reproduction with 26 Plates in Full Color, William Blake. 26 full-color plates from a rare 1826 edition. Includes "The Tyger," "London," "Holy Thursday," and other poems. Printed text of poems. 48pp. 5¼ × 7. 24636-1 Pa. $3.95

OLD-TIME VIGNETTES IN FULL COLOR, Carol Belanger Grafton (ed.). Over 390 charming, often sentimental illustrations, selected from archives of Victorian graphics—pretty women posing, children playing, food, flowers, kittens and puppies, smiling cherubs, birds and butterflies, much more. All copyright-free. 48pp. 9¼ × 12¼. 27269-9 Pa. $5.95

PERSPECTIVE FOR ARTISTS, Rex Vicat Cole. Depth, perspective of sky and sea, shadows, much more, not usually covered. 391 diagrams, 81 reproductions of drawings and paintings. 279pp. 5⅜ × 8½. 22487-2 Pa. $6.95

DRAWING THE LIVING FIGURE, Joseph Sheppard. Innovative approach to artistic anatomy focuses on specifics of surface anatomy, rather than muscles and bones. Over 170 drawings of live models in front, back and side views, and in widely varying poses. Accompanying diagrams. 177 illustrations. Introduction. Index. 144pp. 8⅜ × 11¼. 26723-7 Pa. $7.95

GOTHIC AND OLD ENGLISH ALPHABETS: 100 Complete Fonts, Dan X. Solo. Add power, elegance to posters, signs, other graphics with 100 stunning copyright-free alphabets: Blackstone, Dolbey, Germania, 97 more—including many lower-case, numerals, punctuation marks. 104pp. 8⅛ × 11. 24695-7 Pa. $7.95

HOW TO DO BEADWORK, Mary White. Fundamental book on craft from simple projects to five-bead chains and woven works. 106 illustrations. 142pp. 5⅜ × 8. 20697-1 Pa. $4.95

THE BOOK OF WOOD CARVING, Charles Marshall Sayers. Finest book for beginners discusses fundamentals and offers 34 designs. "Absolutely first rate . . . well thought out and well executed."—E. J. Tangerman. 118pp. 7¾ × 10⅝. 23654-4 Pa. $5.95

ILLUSTRATED CATALOG OF CIVIL WAR MILITARY GOODS: Union Army Weapons, Insignia, Uniform Accessories, and Other Equipment, Schuyler, Hartley, and Graham. Rare, profusely illustrated 1846 catalog includes Union Army uniform and dress regulations, arms and ammunition, coats, insignia, flags, swords, rifles, etc. 226 illustrations. 160pp. 9 × 12. 24939-5 Pa. $10.95

WOMEN'S FASHIONS OF THE EARLY 1900s: An Unabridged Republication of "New York Fashions, 1909," National Cloak & Suit Co. Rare catalog of mail-order fashions documents women's and children's clothing styles shortly after the turn of the century. Captions offer full descriptions, prices. Invaluable resource for fashion, costume historians. Approximately 725 illustrations. 128pp. 8⅜ × 11¼. 27276-1 Pa. $10.95

THE 1912 AND 1915 GUSTAV STICKLEY FURNITURE CATALOGS, Gustav Stickley. With over 200 detailed illustrations and descriptions, these two catalogs are essential reading and reference materials and identification guides for Stickley furniture. Captions cite materials, dimensions and prices. 112pp. 6½ × 9¼. 26676-1 Pa. $9.95

EARLY AMERICAN LOCOMOTIVES, John H. White, Jr. Finest locomotive engravings from early 19th century: historical (1804–74), main-line (after 1870), special, foreign, etc. 147 plates. 142pp. 11⅜ × 8¼. 22772-3 Pa. $8.95

THE TALL SHIPS OF TODAY IN PHOTOGRAPHS, Frank O. Braynard. Lavishly illustrated tribute to nearly 100 majestic contemporary sailing vessels: Amerigo Vespucci, Clearwater, Constitution, Eagle, Mayflower, Sea Cloud, Victory, many more. Authoritative captions provide statistics, background on each ship. 190 black-and-white photographs and illustrations. Introduction. 128pp. 8⅜ × 11¾. 27163-3 Pa. $12.95

EARLY NINETEENTH-CENTURY CRAFTS AND TRADES, Peter Stockham (ed.). Extremely rare 1807 volume describes to youngsters the crafts and trades of the day: brickmaker, weaver, dressmaker, bookbinder, ropemaker, saddler, many more. Quaint prose, charming illustrations for each craft. 20 black-and-white line illustrations. 192pp. 4⅜ × 6. 27293-1 Pa. $4.95

VICTORIAN FASHIONS AND COSTUMES FROM HARPER'S BAZAR, 1867–1898, Stella Blum (ed.). Day costumes, evening wear, sports clothes, shoes, hats, other accessories in over 1,000 detailed engravings. 320pp. 9⅜ × 12¼.
22990-4 Pa. $13.95

GUSTAV STICKLEY, THE CRAFTSMAN, Mary Ann Smith. Superb study surveys broad scope of Stickley's achievement, especially in architecture. Design philosophy, rise and fall of the Craftsman empire, descriptions and floor plans for many Craftsman houses, more. 86 black-and-white halftones. 31 line illustrations. Introduction. 208pp. 6½ × 9¼. 27210-9 Pa. $9.95

THE LONG ISLAND RAIL ROAD IN EARLY PHOTOGRAPHS, Ron Ziel. Over 220 rare photos, informative text document origin (1844) and development of rail service on Long Island. Vintage views of early trains, locomotives, stations, passengers, crews, much more. Captions. 8⅜ × 11¾. 26301-0 Pa. $13.95

THE BOOK OF OLD SHIPS: From Egyptian Galleys to Clipper Ships, Henry B. Culver. Superb, authoritative history of sailing vessels, with 80 magnificent line illustrations. Galley, bark, caravel, longship, whaler, many more. Detailed, informative text on each vessel by noted naval historian. Introduction. 256pp. 5⅜ × 8½. 27332-6 Pa. $6.95

TEN BOOKS ON ARCHITECTURE, Vitruvius. The most important book ever written on architecture. Early Roman aesthetics, technology, classical orders, site selection, all other aspects. Morgan translation. 331pp. 5⅜ × 8½. 20645-9 Pa. $8.95

THE HUMAN FIGURE IN MOTION, Eadweard Muybridge. More than 4,500 stopped-action photos, in action series, showing undraped men, women, children jumping, lying down, throwing, sitting, wrestling, carrying, etc. 390pp. 7⅞ × 10⅝.
20204-6 Clothbd. $24.95

TREES OF THE EASTERN AND CENTRAL UNITED STATES AND CANADA, William M. Harlow. Best one-volume guide to 140 trees. Full descriptions, woodlore, range, etc. Over 600 illustrations. Handy size. 288pp. 4½ × 6⅜.
20395-6 Pa. $5.95

SONGS OF WESTERN BIRDS, Dr. Donald J. Borror. Complete song and call repertoire of 60 western species, including flycatchers, juncoes, cactus wrens, many more—includes fully illustrated booklet. Cassette and manual 99913-0 $8.95

GROWING AND USING HERBS AND SPICES, Milo Miloradovich. Versatile handbook provides all the information needed for cultivation and use of all the herbs and spices available in North America. 4 illustrations. Index. Glossary. 236pp. 5⅜ × 8½. 25058-X Pa. $5.95

BIG BOOK OF MAZES AND LABYRINTHS, Walter Shepherd. 50 mazes and labyrinths in all—classical, solid, ripple, and more—in one great volume. Perfect inexpensive puzzler for clever youngsters. Full solutions. 112pp. 8⅛ × 11.
22951-3 Pa. $3.95

PIANO TUNING, J. Cree Fischer. Clearest, best book for beginner, amateur. Simple repairs, raising dropped notes, tuning by easy method of flattened fifths. No previous skills needed. 4 illustrations. 201pp. 5⅜ × 8½. 23267-0 Pa. $5.95

A SOURCE BOOK IN THEATRICAL HISTORY, A. M. Nagler. Contemporary observers on acting, directing, make-up, costuming, stage props, machinery, scene design, from Ancient Greece to Chekhov. 611pp. 5⅜ × 8½. 20515-0 Pa. $11.95

THE COMPLETE NONSENSE OF EDWARD LEAR, Edward Lear. All nonsense limericks, zany alphabets, Owl and Pussycat, songs, nonsense botany, etc., illustrated by Lear. Total of 320pp. 5⅜ × 8½. (USO) 20167-8 Pa. $5.95

VICTORIAN PARLOUR POETRY: An Annotated Anthology, Michael R. Turner. 117 gems by Longfellow, Tennyson, Browning, many lesser-known poets. "The Village Blacksmith," "Curfew Must Not Ring Tonight," "Only a Baby Small," dozens more, often difficult to find elsewhere. Index of poets, titles, first lines. xxiii + 325pp. 5⅜ × 8¼. 27044-0 Pa. $8.95

DUBLINERS, James Joyce. Fifteen stories offer vivid, tightly focused observations of the lives of Dublin's poorer classes. At least one, "The Dead," is considered a masterpiece. Reprinted complete and unabridged from standard edition. 160pp. 5³⁄₁₆ × 8¼. 26870-5 Pa. $1.00

THE HAUNTED MONASTERY and THE CHINESE MAZE MURDERS, Robert van Gulik. Two full novels by van Gulik, set in 7th-century China, continue adventures of Judge Dee and his companions. An evil Taoist monastery, seemingly supernatural events; overgrown topiary maze hides strange crimes. 27 illustrations. 328pp. 5⅜ × 8½. 23502-5 Pa. $7.95

THE BOOK OF THE SACRED MAGIC OF ABRAMELIN THE MAGE, translated by S. MacGregor Mathers. Medieval manuscript of ceremonial magic. Basic document in Aleister Crowley, Golden Dawn groups. 268pp. 5⅜ × 8½. 23211-5 Pa. $7.95

NEW RUSSIAN-ENGLISH AND ENGLISH-RUSSIAN DICTIONARY, M. A. O'Brien. This is a remarkably handy Russian dictionary, containing a surprising amount of information, including over 70,000 entries. 366pp. 4½ × 6⅛. 20208-9 Pa. $8.95

HISTORIC HOMES OF THE AMERICAN PRESIDENTS, Second, Revised Edition, Irvin Haas. A traveler's guide to American Presidential homes, most open to the public, depicting and describing homes occupied by every American President from George Washington to George Bush. With visiting hours, admission charges, travel routes. 175 photographs. Index. 160pp. 8¼ × 11. 26751-2 Pa. $10.95

NEW YORK IN THE FORTIES, Andreas Feininger. 162 brilliant photographs by the well-known photographer, formerly with *Life* magazine. Commuters, shoppers, Times Square at night, much else from city at its peak. Captions by John von Hartz. 181pp. 9¼ × 10¾. 23585-8 Pa. $12.95

INDIAN SIGN LANGUAGE, William Tomkins. Over 525 signs developed by Sioux and other tribes. Written instructions and diagrams. Also 290 pictographs. 111pp. 6⅛ × 9¼. 22029-X Pa. $3.50

ANATOMY: A Complete Guide for Artists, Joseph Sheppard. A master of figure drawing shows artists how to render human anatomy convincingly. Over 460 illustrations. 224pp. 8⅜ × 11¼. 27279-6 Pa. $9.95

MEDIEVAL CALLIGRAPHY: Its History and Technique, Marc Drogin. Spirited history, comprehensive instruction manual covers 13 styles (ca. 4th century thru 15th). Excellent photographs; directions for duplicating medieval techniques with modern tools. 224pp. 8⅜ × 11¼. 26142-5 Pa. $11.95

DRIED FLOWERS: How to Prepare Them, Sarah Whitlock and Martha Rankin. Complete instructions on how to use silica gel, meal and borax, perlite aggregate, sand and borax, glycerine and water to create attractive permanent flower arrangements. 12 illustrations. 32pp. 5⅜ × 8½. 21802-3 Pa. $1.00

EASY-TO-MAKE BIRD FEEDERS FOR WOODWORKERS, Scott D. Campbell. Detailed, simple-to-use guide for designing, constructing, caring for and using feeders. Text, illustrations for 12 classic and contemporary designs. 96pp. 5⅜ × 8½. 25847-5 Pa. $2.95

OLD-TIME CRAFTS AND TRADES, Peter Stockham. An 1807 book created to teach children about crafts and trades open to them as future careers. It describes in detailed, nontechnical terms 24 different occupations, among them coachmaker, gardener, hairdresser, lacemaker, shoemaker, wheelwright, copper-plate printer, milliner, trunkmaker, merchant and brewer. Finely detailed engravings illustrate each occupation. 192pp. 4⅝ × 6. 27398-9 Pa. $4.95

THE HISTORY OF UNDERCLOTHES, C. Willett Cunnington and Phyllis Cunnington. Fascinating, well-documented survey covering six centuries of English undergarments, enhanced with over 100 illustrations: 12th-century laced-up bodice, footed long drawers (1795), 19th-century bustles, 19th-century corsets for men, Victorian "bust improvers," much more. 272pp. 5⅜ × 8¼. 27124-2 Pa. $9.95

ARTS AND CRAFTS FURNITURE: The Complete Brooks Catalog of 1912, Brooks Manufacturing Co. Photos and detailed descriptions of more than 150 now very collectible furniture designs from the Arts and Crafts movement depict davenports, settees, buffets, desks, tables, chairs, bedsteads, dressers and more, all built of solid, quarter-sawed oak. Invaluable for students and enthusiasts of antiques, Americana and the decorative arts. 80pp. 6½ × 9¼. 27471-3 Pa. $7.95

HOW WE INVENTED THE AIRPLANE: An Illustrated History, Orville Wright. Fascinating firsthand account covers early experiments, construction of planes and motors, first flights, much more. Introduction and commentary by Fred C. Kelly. 76 photographs. 96pp. 8¼ × 11. 25662-6 Pa. $7.95

THE ARTS OF THE SAILOR: Knotting, Splicing and Ropework, Hervey Garrett Smith. Indispensable shipboard reference covers tools, basic knots and useful hitches; handsewing and canvas work, more. Over 100 illustrations. Delightful reading for sea lovers. 256pp. 5⅜ × 8½. 26440-8 Pa. $7.95

FRANK LLOYD WRIGHT'S FALLINGWATER: The House and Its History, Second, Revised Edition, Donald Hoffmann. A total revision—both in text and illustrations—of the standard document on Fallingwater, the boldest, most personal architectural statement of Wright's mature years, updated with valuable new material from the recently opened Frank Lloyd Wright Archives. "Fascinating"—*The New York Times*. 116 illustrations. 128pp. 9¼ × 10¾.
27430-6 Pa. $10.95

PHOTOGRAPHIC SKETCHBOOK OF THE CIVIL WAR, Alexander Gardner. 100 photos taken on field during the Civil War. Famous shots of Manassas, Harper's Ferry, Lincoln, Richmond, slave pens, etc. 244pp. 10⅛ × 8¼.
22731-6 Pa. $9.95

FIVE ACRES AND INDEPENDENCE, Maurice G. Kains. Great back-to-the-land classic explains basics of self-sufficient farming. The one book to get. 95 illustrations. 397pp. 5⅜ × 8½.
20974-1 Pa. $6.95

SONGS OF EASTERN BIRDS, Dr. Donald J. Borror. Songs and calls of 60 species most common to eastern U.S.: warblers, woodpeckers, flycatchers, thrushes, larks, many more in high-quality recording.
Cassette and manual 99912-2 $8.95

A MODERN HERBAL, Margaret Grieve. Much the fullest, most exact, most useful compilation of herbal material. Gigantic alphabetical encyclopedia, from aconite to zedoary, gives botanical information, medical properties, folklore, economic uses, much else. Indispensable to serious reader. 161 illustrations. 888pp. 6½ × 9¼.
2-vol. set. (USO)
Vol. I: 22798-7 Pa. $9.95
Vol. II: 22799-5 Pa. $9.95

HIDDEN TREASURE MAZE BOOK, Dave Phillips. Solve 34 challenging mazes accompanied by heroic tales of adventure. Evil dragons, people-eating plants, bloodthirsty giants, many more dangerous adversaries lurk at every twist and turn. 34 mazes, stories, solutions. 48pp. 8¼ × 11.
24566-7 Pa. $2.95

LETTERS OF W. A. MOZART, Wolfgang A. Mozart. Remarkable letters show bawdy wit, humor, imagination, musical insights, contemporary musical world; includes some letters from Leopold Mozart. 276pp. 5⅜ × 8½.
22859-2 Pa. $6.95

BASIC PRINCIPLES OF CLASSICAL BALLET, Agrippina Vaganova. Great Russian theoretician, teacher explains methods for teaching classical ballet. 118 illustrations. 175pp. 5⅜ × 8½.
22036-2 Pa. $4.95

THE JUMPING FROG, Mark Twain. Revenge edition. The original story of The Celebrated Jumping Frog of Calaveras County, a hapless French translation, and Twain's hilarious "retranslation" from the French. 12 illustrations. 66pp. 5⅜ × 8½.
22686-7 Pa. $3.50

BEST REMEMBERED POEMS, Martin Gardner (ed.). The 126 poems in this superb collection of 19th- and 20th-century British and American verse range from Shelley's "To a Skylark" to the impassioned "Renascence" of Edna St. Vincent Millay and to Edward Lear's whimsical "The Owl and the Pussycat." 224pp. 5⅜ × 8½.
27165-X Pa. $4.95

COMPLETE SONNETS, William Shakespeare. Over 150 exquisite poems deal with love, friendship, the tyranny of time, beauty's evanescence, death and other themes in language of remarkable power, precision and beauty. Glossary of archaic terms. 80pp. 5³⁄₁₆ × 8¼.
26686-9 Pa. $1.00

BODIES IN A BOOKSHOP, R. T. Campbell. Challenging mystery of blackmail and murder with ingenious plot and superbly drawn characters. In the best tradition of British suspense fiction. 192pp. 5⅜ × 8½.
24720-1 Pa. $5.95

THE WIT AND HUMOR OF OSCAR WILDE, Alvin Redman (ed.). More than 1,000 ripostes, paradoxes, wisecracks: Work is the curse of the drinking classes; I can resist everything except temptation; etc. 258pp. 5⅜ × 8½. 20602-5 Pa. $4.95

SHAKESPEARE LEXICON AND QUOTATION DICTIONARY, Alexander Schmidt. Full definitions, locations, shades of meaning in every word in plays and poems. More than 50,000 exact quotations. 1,485pp. 6½ × 9¼. 2-vol. set.
Vol. 1: 22726-X Pa. $15.95
Vol. 2: 22727-8 Pa. $15.95

SELECTED POEMS, Emily Dickinson. Over 100 best-known, best-loved poems by one of America's foremost poets, reprinted from authoritative early editions. No comparable edition at this price. Index of first lines. 64pp. 5³/₁₆ × 8¼.
26466-1 Pa. $1.00

CELEBRATED CASES OF JUDGE DEE (DEE GOONG AN), translated by Robert van Gulik. Authentic 18th-century Chinese detective novel; Dee and associates solve three interlocked cases. Led to van Gulik's own stories with same characters. Extensive introduction. 9 illustrations. 237pp. 5⅜ × 8½.
23337-5 Pa. $5.95

THE MALLEUS MALEFICARUM OF KRAMER AND SPRENGER, translated by Montague Summers. Full text of most important witchhunter's "bible," used by both Catholics and Protestants. 278pp. 6⅝ × 10. 22802-9 Pa. $10.95

SPANISH STORIES/CUENTOS ESPAÑOLES: A Dual-Language Book, Angel Flores (ed.). Unique format offers 13 great stories in Spanish by Cervantes, Borges, others. Faithful English translations on facing pages. 352pp. 5⅜ × 8½.
25399-6 Pa. $8.95

THE CHICAGO WORLD'S FAIR OF 1893: A Photographic Record, Stanley Appelbaum (ed.). 128 rare photos show 200 buildings, Beaux-Arts architecture, Midway, original Ferris Wheel, Edison's kinetoscope, more. Architectural emphasis; full text. 116pp. 8¼ × 11. 23990-X Pa. $9.95

OLD QUEENS, N.Y., IN EARLY PHOTOGRAPHS, Vincent F. Seyfried and William Asadorian. Over 160 rare photographs of Maspeth, Jamaica, Jackson Heights, and other areas. Vintage views of DeWitt Clinton mansion, 1939 World's Fair and more. Captions. 192pp. 8⅞ × 11. 26358-4 Pa. $12.95

CAPTURED BY THE INDIANS: 15 Firsthand Accounts, 1750–1870, Frederick Drimmer. Astounding true historical accounts of grisly torture, bloody conflicts, relentless pursuits, miraculous escapes and more, by people who lived to tell the tale. 384pp. 5⅜ × 8½. 24901-8 Pa. $7.95

THE WORLD'S GREAT SPEECHES, Lewis Copeland and Lawrence W. Lamm (eds.). Vast collection of 278 speeches of Greeks to 1970. Powerful and effective models; unique look at history. 842pp. 5⅜ × 8½. 20468-5 Pa. $13.95

THE BOOK OF THE SWORD, Sir Richard F. Burton. Great Victorian scholar/adventurer's eloquent, erudite history of the "queen of weapons"—from prehistory to early Roman Empire. Evolution and development of early swords, variations (sabre, broadsword, cutlass, scimitar, etc.), much more. 336pp. 6⅛ × 9¼. 25434-8 Pa. $8.95

AUTOBIOGRAPHY: The Story of My Experiments with Truth, Mohandas K. Gandhi. Boyhood, legal studies, purification, the growth of the Satyagraha (nonviolent protest) movement. Critical, inspiring work of the man responsible for the freedom of India. 480pp. 5⅜ × 8½. (USO) 24593-4 Pa. $7.95

CELTIC MYTHS AND LEGENDS, T. W. Rolleston. Masterful retelling of Irish and Welsh stories and tales. Cuchulain, King Arthur, Deirdre, the Grail, many more. First paperback edition. 58 full-page illustrations. 512pp. 5⅜ × 8½.
 26507-2 Pa. $9.95

THE PRINCIPLES OF PSYCHOLOGY, William James. Famous long course complete, unabridged. Stream of thought, time perception, memory, experimental methods; great work decades ahead of its time. 94 figures. 1,391pp. 5⅜ × 8½. 2-vol. set.
 Vol. I: 20381-6 Pa. $12.95
 Vol. II: 20382-4 Pa. $12.95

THE WORLD AS WILL AND REPRESENTATION, Arthur Schopenhauer. Definitive English translation of Schopenhauer's life work, correcting more than 1,000 errors, omissions in earlier translations. Translated by E. F. J. Payne. Total of 1,269pp. 5⅜ × 8½. 2-vol. set. Vol. 1: 21761-2 Pa. $10.95
 Vol. 2: 21762-0 Pa. $11.95

MAGIC AND MYSTERY IN TIBET, Madame Alexandra David-Neel. Experiences among lamas, magicians, sages, sorcerers, Bonpa wizards. A true psychic discovery. 32 illustrations. 321pp. 5⅜ × 8½. (USO) 22682-4 Pa. $8.95

THE EGYPTIAN BOOK OF THE DEAD, E. A. Wallis Budge. Complete reproduction of Ani's papyrus, finest ever found. Full hieroglyphic text, interlinear transliteration, word-for-word translation, smooth translation. 533pp. 6½ × 9¼.
 21866-X Pa. $9.95

MATHEMATICS FOR THE NONMATHEMATICIAN, Morris Kline. Detailed, college-level treatment of mathematics in cultural and historical context, with numerous exercises. Recommended Reading Lists. Tables. Numerous figures. 641pp. 5⅜ × 8½. 24823-2 Pa. $11.95

THEORY OF WING SECTIONS: Including a Summary of Airfoil Data, Ira H. Abbott and A. E. von Doenhoff. Concise compilation of subsonic aerodynamic characteristics of NACA wing sections, plus description of theory. 350pp. of tables. 693pp. 5⅜ × 8½. 60586-8 Pa. $13.95

THE RIME OF THE ANCIENT MARINER, Gustave Doré, S. T. Coleridge. Doré's finest work; 34 plates capture moods, subtleties of poem. Flawless full-size reproductions printed on facing pages with authoritative text of poem. "Beautiful. Simply beautiful."—*Publisher's Weekly.* 77pp. 9¼ × 12. 22305-1 Pa. $5.95

NORTH AMERICAN INDIAN DESIGNS FOR ARTISTS AND CRAFTS-PEOPLE, Eva Wilson. Over 360 authentic copyright-free designs adapted from Navajo blankets, Hopi pottery, Sioux buffalo hides, more. Geometrics, symbolic figures, plant and animal motifs, etc. 128pp. 8⅜ × 11. (EUK) 25341-4 Pa. $7.95

SCULPTURE: Principles and Practice, Louis Slobodkin. Step-by-step approach to clay, plaster, metals, stone; classical and modern. 253 drawings, photos. 255pp. 8¼ × 11. 22960-2 Pa. $9.95

THE INFLUENCE OF SEA POWER UPON HISTORY, 1660–1783, A. T. Mahan. Influential classic of naval history and tactics still used as text in war colleges. First paperback edition. 4 maps. 24 battle plans. 640pp. 5⅜ × 8½.
25509-3 Pa. $12.95

THE STORY OF THE TITANIC AS TOLD BY ITS SURVIVORS, Jack Winocour (ed.). What it was really like. Panic, despair, shocking inefficiency, and a little heroism. More thrilling than any fictional account. 26 illustrations. 320pp. 5⅜ × 8½.
20610-6 Pa. $7.95

FAIRY AND FOLK TALES OF THE IRISH PEASANTRY, William Butler Yeats (ed.). Treasury of 64 tales from the twilight world of Celtic myth and legend: "The Soul Cages," "The Kildare Pooka," "King O'Toole and his Goose," many more. Introduction and Notes by W. B. Yeats. 352pp. 5⅜ × 8½.
26941-8 Pa. $7.95

BUDDHIST MAHAYANA TEXTS, E. B. Cowell and Others (eds.). Superb, accurate translations of basic documents in Mahayana Buddhism, highly important in history of religions. The Buddha-karita of Asvaghosha, Larger Sukhavativyuha, more. 448pp. 5⅜ × 8½. ,
25552-2 Pa. $9.95

ONE TWO THREE . . . INFINITY: Facts and Speculations of Science, George Gamow. Great physicist's fascinating, readable overview of contemporary science: number theory, relativity, fourth dimension, entropy, genes, atomic structure, much more. 128 illustrations. Index. 352pp. 5⅜ × 8½.
25664-2 Pa. $8.95

ENGINEERING IN HISTORY, Richard Shelton Kirby, et al. Broad, nontechnical survey of history's major technological advances: birth of Greek science, industrial revolution, electricity and applied science, 20th-century automation, much more. 181 illustrations. ". . . excellent . . ."—Isis. Bibliography. vii + 530pp. 5⅜ × 8¼.
26412-2 Pa. $14.95

Prices subject to change without notice.
Available at your book dealer or write for free catalog to Dept. GI, Dover Publications, Inc., 31 East 2nd St., Mineola, N.Y. 11501. Dover publishes more than 500 books each year on science, elementary and advanced mathematics, biology, music, art, literary history, social sciences and other areas.